CASE STUDIES IN
CULTURAL ANTHROPOLOGY

GENERAL EDITORS

George and Louise Spindler

STANFORD UNIVERSITY

JONES, David E. **Sanapia; Comanche medicine woman.** Holt, Rinehart and Winston, 1972. 107p il map bibl (Case studies in cultural anthropology) 73-179548. 2.75 pa. ISBN 0-03-088456-X

CHOICE   MAR. '73

Sociology & Anthropology

Through the medium of a well-written life history of an older medicine woman, Jones delves into Comanche shamanism, witchcraft, and ghost sickness especially as found in contemporary Comanche life. The central figure is Sanapia — her life, attitudes, religious beliefs, medicine activities, and paraphernalia. Unlike most life histories, Sanapia's life is placed within both an historical and social setting which provides greater understanding as to her role as a medicine woman. Of interest is the way in which she combines the potentially conflicting beliefs of Christianity, peyotism, and traditional Comanche religion. As a life history, it may be comparable to Nancy Lurie's *Mountain wolf woman* (1961); as an ethnography, it supplements and adds new data to Ernest Wallace and E. A. Hoebel's *The Comanches; lords of the South Plains* (1952). Recommended for all high school and college libraries. One map; 13 pictures.

SANAPIA

Comanche Medicine Woman

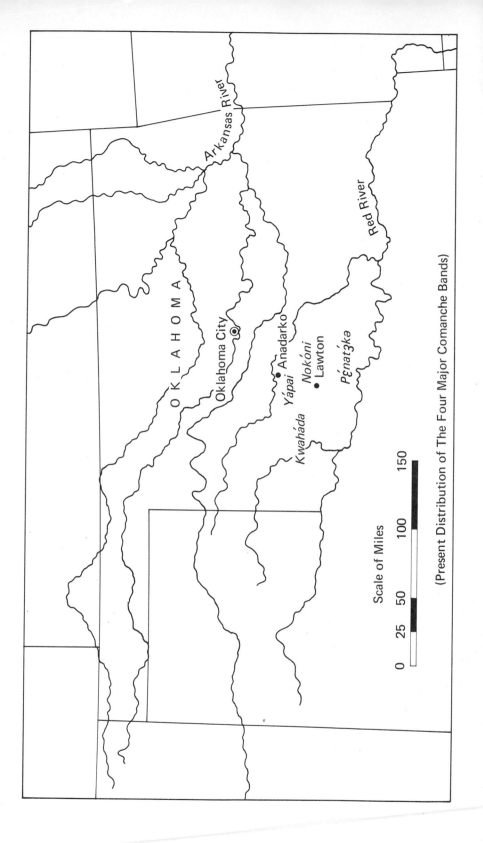

Scale of Miles

0   25   50   100   150

(Present Distribution of The Four Major Comanche Bands)

SANAPIA

Comanche Medicine Woman

By

DAVID E. JONES

The University of Oklahoma

HOLT, RINEHART AND WINSTON

NEW YORK   CHICAGO   SAN FRANCISCO   ATLANTA
DALLAS   MONTREAL   TORONTO   LONDON   SYDNEY

Cover: *Sanapia, 1968*

FOR MARY, JOEY, AND SHAY

Foreword

About the Series

These case studies in cultural anthropology are designed to bring to students in the social sciences insights into the richness and complexity of human life as it is lived in different ways and in different places. They are written by men and women who have lived in the societies they write about, and who are professionally trained as observers and interpreters of human behavior. The authors are also teachers, and in writing their books they have kept the students who will read them foremost in their minds. It is our belief that when an understanding of a way of life very different from one's own is gained, abstractions and generalizations about social structure, cultural values, subsistence techniques, and other universal categories of human social behavior become meaningful.

About the Author

David E. Jones received his B.A. in anthropology from the University of North Carolina in 1966, and his M.A. from the University of Oklahoma in 1968. At present he is completing his doctoral dissertation for the University of Oklahoma under a Woodrow Wilson Dissertation Fellowship.

The field research upon which this book is based was accomplished over a three-year period beginning in 1967. During the first year of fieldwork, the author was employed by the Doris Duke Indian Oral History Project, American Indian Institute, University of Oklahoma. Much of the taped and transcribed interview material utilized in the compilation of this book is at present in the files of the Oral History Project at the University of Oklahoma.

Mr. Jones has published several articles on the ethnopharmacopeia of the Comanche Indians.

About the Book

As the author writes, this case study is an ethnographic portrait of Sanapia, Comanche medicine woman. With an abundance of firsthand accounts and on the scene observations, the author assists the reader in understanding the complex role of a Comanche Eagle doctor. Jones attempts to describe every aspect of Sanapia's role, including detailed accounts of her ritual behavior, her attitude toward her profession, the paraphernalia she employs, and her function in Comanche society.

The study is special in that Sanapia is the last surviving Comanche Eagle doctor. Ethnographic materials and popular materials on the colorful Comanche raiders are available, but very little has been previously recorded on the institution of the Comanche traditional doctor.

Jones was able to obtain his excellent data as the adopted son of Sanapia. As he explains, this close association had disadvantages as well as advantages. It was assumed, for example, that as Sanapia's son, the author would automatically know many of the obvious aspects of the doctor's role. Furthermore, the role of "Young Son" carried with it a series of complex, reciprocal role relations.

The reader is given intimate details concerning Sanapia's training, which was lengthy and complex. After the final rituals involved in receiving the Power necessary for an Eagle doctor, Sanapia had to be passed on separately by four different instructors.

One unique chapter is devoted to the detailed preparation of herbal medicines and methods of administering them. The illnesses treated ranged from heart pain, pneumonia, and paralysis to exzema and loss of appetite.

Since Sanapia spent a great deal of time treating "ghost-sickness," the author explains the meaning of the concept and describes the symptoms and treatment. Jones analyzes the psychogenic roots of this disease, considered by the Comanche to be peculiar to the "Indian." The author believes the malady may be viewed as a conversion reaction related to unmanageable psychic stresses.

The author attributes Sanapia's success as an Eagle doctor to the fact that she was able to adapt quickly to the changes taking place in Comanche culture. This process of adaptation was simplified for Sanapia as her own home environment had required that she adjust to three disparate religious systems—the Christianity of her father, the Peyotism of her uncle and paternal grandfather, and the Plains Indian pattern of vision quests and guardian spirit represented by her mother, the Eagle doctor.

Upon completing the reading of the detailed study of Sanapia's training and role behaviors, the reader feels that he knows Sanapia more intimately than do her own peers.

GEORGE *and* LOUISE SPINDLER
General Editors

Portola Valley, Calif.

Acknowledgments and Comments

Transcriptions of tape-recorded interviews in English enabled me to present extensive verbatim material from Sanapia and my other informants. In order to sustain the tone and manner of the original response, I attempted no editing of these passages. All quoted material, unless otherwise designated, is after Sanapia (pseudonym). Also, no attempt has been made to touch up the old photographs of Sanapia and her family.

I would like to express my appreciation to Dr. William E. Bittle of the Department of Anthropology of the University of Oklahoma for his valuable advice, criticism, and support during the development of this study; to Dr. Morris E. Opler of the Department of Anthropology of the University of Oklahoma for his encouragement and aid toward the publication of this book; and to Dr. George J. Goodman of the Department of Botany of the University of Oklahoma for his enthusiastic assistance in the identification of the medicinal plants discussed in Chapter 3. My most profound respect and appreciation must go to Sanapia, who gave me her trust and active intelligent assistance throughout the period of my fieldwork among the Comanche people of southwestern Oklahoma. It is her wish that this be the book of her "medicine way," and I hope that I have succeeded.

DAVID E. JONES

Norman, Oklahoma

Pronunciation Guide

The following is a key to the pronunciation of Comanche words appearing in the text.

ə   Pronounced like *e* in over, under.

ɔ   Pronounced like *o* in horn, fork.

ɜ   Pronounced like *u* in fur, turn.

ɛ   Pronounced like *a* in bare, care.

β   This sound can be approximated by compressing the lips for the pronunciation of a *b* sound and proceeding to pronounce a *v* sound.

:   Indicates the lengthening of the preceding vowel sound.

Contents

Introduction

T HE ETHNOGRAPHIC IMMORTALITY of the Comanches rests almost exclusively
on the data obtained and published by the members of the 1933 Ethnol-
ogical Field Study Group of the Santa Fe Laboratory of Anthropology.
Several members of this group, notably Ralph Linton and E. Adamson Hoebel,
have produced valuable contributions to the knowledge and understanding of
Comanche culture. The institution of the Comanche traditional doctor, however,
was only superficially recorded by the members of the Santa Fe group and even
less satisfactorily recorded in earlier and less rigorous accounts of the Comanches.
It is because of the paucity of material in this area and because of a unique set
of circumstances which enabled me to achieve an unusually close rapport with
the only traditional Medicine woman now functioning in Comanche society that
I attempted to fill some of the aforementioned void with an intensive study of
this doctor.

This study will be an ethnographic portrait of Sanapia, Comanche Medicine woman. The attempt will be made to describe every possible aspect and facet
of her role as Medicine woman and to consider her social position and cultural
meaning in the context of contemporary Comanche society. It is hoped that the
method of presentation employed in this book will enable the reader not only to
understand how a Comanche Medicine woman performs the prescribed behavior
and ritual of her role, her attitudes toward her profession, the paraphernalia she
employs, and her function in Comanche society but also to gain insight into the
personality and character of the woman who is the last surviving Comanche eagle
doctor.

Supernaturalism is often an extremely difficult area of culture for the
ethnographer to approach with any degree of depth or intimacy. This situation
becomes exaggerated, as in the case of the Comanches, when certain supernaturalistic institutions are considered by the members of the culture as final bulwarks of
traditional values, or last vestiges of a "golden era." When these institutions are of
a kind to elicit negative responses from the dominant culture in a situation of

1

ongoing acculturation, or when they are in real or imagined conflict with similar institutions in the culture in dominance, they become even more elusive to the ethnographer. For example, Sanapia's initial resistance to converse on the subject of native doctoring practices was based on her fear of ridicule and her belief that information which she gave this investigator could make her liable to arrest for practicing medicine without a license.

My first experience with other Comanche informants on the subject of Comanche native doctors was similar. Though many were fonts of knowledge on practically any subject touched upon in the preliminaries of an interview, my questions concerning even such an inoffensive subject as the existence of living native doctors were met with terse denials. It was only after establishing a socially visible rapport with Sanapia that I found the first resistance on this subject to subside. I was then able to obtain information from certain informants who had been Sanapia's patients or who at least had some comments to offer on the subject of Sanapia, native doctors, or supernaturalism in general.

The term "medicine," when used by Sanapia, refers specifically to material items which are a necessary part of her activities when she is involved in manipulating or directing her personal *puha*, or supernatural power. *Puha* is equivalent to the terms "Medicine" and "power." Sanapia uses the term "doctoring" to mean any kind of action by a *puhakut*, or one who possesses an extraordinary degree of supernatural power, which is concerned with the direction of Medicine at another for purposes of good or evil.

Because of the dearth of material on Comanche culture, I have but a minimal amount of very general information with which to compare the sometimes highly detailed data obtained from Sanapia on the intricacies of her profession. With comparative literary precedent lacking on this specific subject and in the absence of other doctors similar in kind to Sanapia, this study must be considered as a discussion of the "Medicine way" of *a* Comanche Medicine woman. Generalizations on certain Comanche supernaturalistic notions will be made only when a number of informants have been in acceptable accord. It should be noted that even if there existed a more complete literature on Comanche doctors, and if there existed at present Medicine women with which to compare Sanapia, generic statements on the subject would still be artificial and tenuous, given the great degree of latitude granted the individual doctor in the details of the performance of his role and the individualistic bent of Comanche personality in general (Wallace and Hoebel 1952:155; Kardiner 1945:81).

The bias of the ethnographer is always a crucial element in determining the outcome of his field research and the conclusions which he will draw from such experience. I refer to personal bias, partiality, inclination, or prejudice not specifically concerned with a field problem. Of course, it is ideally desirable that the field researcher have as little bias as possible, but he will necessarily possess a certain way of viewing given situations and individuals and, whether he desires to or not, he will judge them. Both for the ethnographer's sake and for the sake of his reader in evaluating his product, I feel that the researcher should attempt to make as explicit as possible the particular manner in which he viewed his subjects, any partiality he experienced, and the manner in which he feels he was accepted by his subjects. Especially with a book of this kind, this is necessary since so much of the material upon which this study was based came from a single informant. The particular relationship which I experienced with Sanapia doubtless colored the kinds of information which I obtained from her.

There was both an age and a sex difference between Sanapia and me, besides the obvious cultural differences. The rapidity with which she adopted me into her household was as cumbersome as it was helpful, for by this stroke I lost many of the advantages which formalized interviewing can lend, while gaining the advantages of confidences and a relative invisibility. She adopted me as her son and in so doing promoted an imbalance in our relationship in which she was in the position to demand more of me than I was of her. This relationship gave me the opportunity to gather much information concerning her attitudes and sentiments relating to her self-concept and her view of herself in relation to Comanche society as a whole, while it was more difficult to gather those kinds of data dealing with the more overt and obvious aspects of her role. She seemed to feel that by the simple fact of adopting me I would know all the necessary premises, and she would react irritably when I would question her on those subjects about which she felt I already knew. Also, by being classified as a "young son," *tuiβitsi*, I was expected to interact more with her sons, grandson, and nephews and to maintain a respect–distance from Sanapia.

The sex difference was not as important as the age difference since Sanapia,

Sanapia and the author.

being a *puhakut*, considered herself equal to a male. However, I did notice that females who interviewed Sanapia were able to gather information of a much different nature than I was able to obtain. The differences were not crucial, but mainly differences of tone and level. Because of the social position in which she felt herself to be, she tended to "talk down" to females, while she would converse with me as a social equal.

The fact that I was so closely associated with Sanapia and her family also tended to affect my relationship with other Comanches. I was not reacted to as a harmless and innocuous outsider. I was Sanapia's "friend" or "son." Consequently, Sanapia's sympathizers would be overly gracious in discussions, while her enemies would be unduly harsh. It was often difficult to retain control in an interview. This entire situation was aggravated because Sanapia, perhaps because of her role as a *puhakut*, was more apt to draw an emotional rather than a rational reaction.

Naturally, because of my close association with the northern bands, I was found highly suspect by the southern Comanche bands. I must admit that I had less personal sympathy for the southern band members, possibly because of my initial enculturation by the northerners. This may have made me more susceptible to identify the cleavage in Comanche society between northern and southern "tribes." I attempted to guard my emotions in this area by establishing historical roots for the divisions in Comanche society and by offering rationalizations for my major use of northern informants. The bulk of my data comes from *Yapai* and *Kwahada* band members; for the most part, these are the Comanches of whom I speak.

Sanapia is approaching the last days of her career as doctor and is beginning to prepare for the training of her successor. She views this study as the book of her Medicine way and feels that if she should die before she is able to complete the training of her successor, this book will act to complete the training.

I'm going to give him [Sanapia's grandson] all that. He might not keep it up, but he'll have those medicines to work with. I'm going to make him understand too. You [referring to the author] got to write down all those medicines what I tell you . . . write it on a book and keep it until he gets old enough. If I'm still living two or three years, well, if I pass away then you could just tell him that . . . just give him what you taking down.

1

The Comanches

Historical Background

THE WORD "COMANCHE" first appeared shortly after 1700 in the records of the colonial administration of the Spanish settlements in the vicinity of Santa Fe, New Mexico. For a long while the etymology of the word was not fully understood since no similar root appeared in the Spanish language. In 1943 some light was thrown on this problem by Marvin K. Opler, in his article "The Origin of Comanche and Ute," who reported that *komanticia* was a Ute word for "enemy." It was applied by the Utes to the Comanche, Arapaho, Cheyenne, and Kiowa before 1726. After this period the Comanches became the major enemies of the Utes, and the word became specifically applied to them. The Comanches were first introduced to the Spanish in New Mexico by the Utes, and thus the word entered the Spanish language from which it was later borrowed into English as "Comanche."

The Comanches are speakers of the Uto-Aztecan language family in much the same sense as the English-speaking peoples are members of the Indo-European language family. The Uto-Aztecan group is divided into three major branches— Shoshonean, Sonoran, and Nahuatlan. The Shoshonean speakers are centered in the Great Basin regions of western North America. The Shoshonean branch can be further divided into Ute-Chemehuevi, Mano-Bannock, and Shoshone-Comanche. The northern Shoshone and Comanche languages are mutually intelligible, and the differences that exist rest on slight phonetic shifts, not in grammatical structure or form. My Comanche informants noted that the Shoshone Indians speak "Comanche"; however, they speak it rapidly and cut vocalization of their words short. It is from the great similarity in the Comanche and Shoshone languages that the derivation of the Comanche from a Shoshonean parent stock is posited by most authors.

5

Comanche Origin

The Comanches' emergence probably occurred on the eastern fringes of the Basin area, somewhere in the vicinity of southwestern Montana and northwestern Wyoming. The specific area of Comanche birth would be impossible to pinpoint; however, judging from the range of the eastern Shoshone, the origin tales of the Comanches, and the Spanish records of New Spain, it can be suggested that the area of Wyoming between the Yellowstone and Platte Rivers may come close to defining the general vicinity of Comanche origin.

The most commonly recorded tale of Comanche origin tells of a dispute which arose among a large group of Indians who were traveling in the northwestern Wyoming area. Two factions of this group disagreed over the division of a game animal, usually identified as a bear. As a result, they separated. One group went north, and this group is now identified as the Shoshone. The other group turned south and east, and the tale states that this group was the Comanche.

The following is Sanapia's version of the origin of the Comanches. I include it here because it is an explanation of Comanche origin which to my knowledge has never been recorded and also because it illustrates a significant point with reference to Sanapia. The core reason for the eventual fracturing of the main group is attributed to disease. This type of explanation would seem most relevant to Sanapia as a doctor. This tale was taught to Sanapia by her mother, who in turn learned it from her father.

There was lots of groups of them at that time . . . by the thousands, here and there, just like that. They be on a river, east of those big mountains . . . Wyoming, I guess. This whole army of Indians, mens, womens, and childrens. Somehow, I don't know how, they got a big sickness. It was this polio . . . something like that stuff, I think. Did you ever hear the like of that? It just twist their arms and their legs this way and that way. It twist their necks too. They act like that for about five minutes, and they just die. If they walking, fall right over and die where they are. The bottom of that place where they were camping was just full of dead peoples. So this man, like a chief or something, got on his horse and rode around the camp and he was talking loud, you know. He said, "I want you all, this group, go south as far as you could go. If you don't, you are going to all die out soon." Then they all got on their horses with their wives and childrens and just left their tepee there or what they living in, them days. They just took out carrying nothing except their knives. They didn't even have nothing to carry water in. So that big camp went south just as far as they could go. Then that man said to some other people, "Now you all go west . . . right straight west just as far as you can go. When you come to the big mountains just go on the other side if you could get over. You other group, go northwest, way up that way. It'll be alright." And so they scattered like that . . . all those ways. Some of them was left and they said, "We going east." The chief said, No, don't go that way. That's white people's land. They be up that way when you get over there. They going to kill you all. You all go west just so far. When you hit a river just live there." So these other folks went southwest from there and northwest. They all scattered and went like that. These other ones that didn't believe him, well, they just died. Their bodies were everywhere. So lot of them end up in the mountains. Bunch went into Wyoming, I guess, and another bunch went back into Texas somewhere and they all went separate there. And now these, I forgot what their name is . . . way up in southwest of California, I think. Well, they talk like us. I don't know their white man name but us Indians call them ʒkai. That has meaning of "red Comanches." That's what their name is. Then over there in Utah there's a bunch talk like us, and they talk easy, slow, say every word like us Comanches. They call us word means something like "they come from hot country." You know, some folks tell you that Comanches come from Mexico, but it ain't true. Comanches been here and there but they come from up north somewhere. My folks, as far as they can remember, come from Colorado near Denver somewhere, but it wasn't no Denver in them days. The army run my folks and their folks in Oklahoma, but we didn't belong here way back. We from Colorado. That's where my father's father was killed by them Utes. I still know that country from what the old people told me and what I ask them.

Migrations

In the late 1600s the Comanches began to migrate southward into contact with the Spanish settlements of New Spain and east onto the Plains. The Comanches most likely moved south to be nearer a source of horses, which they first acquired raiding with the Utes in northern New Mexico. The first large group of Comanches appeared in the New Mexico area around 1705. In the succeeding ten or fifteen years, with the Utes, they were constant sources of harassment to the Spanish settlements in the area. In approximately 1726, the Comanches, perhaps feeling their new power with the acquisition of the horse, turned on their former allies, the Utes. Many of the war stories told by Sanapia and some of my older Comanche informants tell of horse-raiding expeditions against the Utes.

In the early eighteenth century the Comanches began to expand to a greater degree onto the Plains. The contraction of the pedestrian Dismal River culture in the central Plains around 1725 is attributed by some authors to the energized predatory equestrian Comanche people. By the middle of the eighteenth century the Comanches had established themselves as a real threat to the Spanish settlements in New Mexico. At first, however, the Spanish policy toward the Comanches was relatively long-suffering because the existence of the mounted and war-like Comanches acted as a protective barrier on New Spain's eastern frontiers against intrusion from that direction by large numbers of French and English. During this period, however, the Comanches made treaties with certain tribes to the north who were sympathetic to the French, and thus French traders began to supply the Comanches with firearms, a trade item which the Spanish had always feared to release to the Comanches. In the late eighteenth century the dangerous situation provoked by the Comanche's acquisition of guns stimulated the Spanish to send military forces against the Comanches, whose center at that time was in southeastern Colorado. In approximately 1790 the northern Comanche bands, perhaps responding to the military pressures imposed by the Spanish, made an alliance with the Kiowa, an alliance which was never broken.

In 1820 Major Long encountered a large camp of Comanches on the upper great bend of the Arkansas River. Prior to this time the Comanches had little contact with the Anglo-Americans. In the latter part of the eighteen century and the early nineteenth century the Comanches had moved into an area which would roughly encompass southeastern Colorado, southwestern Kansas, central and western Oklahoma, and northern Texas. In fact, in 1834 General Leavenworth and Colonel Dodge met with a large encampment of northern Comanches about 10 miles north of Fort Sill, Oklahoma, on Chandler Creek within a mile of where Sanapia's house now stands.

Relationship to Shoshone

To gain a full appreciation of the roots of historical and contemporary Comanche society, two important phenomena must be considered—the Shoshonean basis of Comanche culture and the effects of the acquisition of the horse and the subsequent "plainsification" of this Shoshonean base culture. Since the similarities which the Comanches share with other Plains tribes are obvious, these will not be exhaustively discussed. Emphasis will be placed on those cultural traits which differentiate the Comanches from other Indian groups of the Plains and which illustrate Shoshonean influences in Comanche culture.

The physiography of the generic eastern Shoshonean habitat can be described as a Basin-Range type, an area of high, arid semidesert with sagebrush and juniper as the predominant floral cover (Kroeber 1939:798). This environment, in its relative meagerness, presented difficulties for peoples who attempted to inhabit it. Subsistence was gained mainly from gathering; seed, bulb, and root collecting; and small-game hunting in the southeastern Basin-Range area. The land could not support a large group of people in one place for any length of time. Therefore, the pattern of small nomadic bands was necessitated. There was no clan organization. Residence after marriage depended on which family had the greatest food surplus at the time. There was no bride price, and marriages were generally unstable, the partners separating at will. Fraternal wife lending occurred, as well as the customary marriage of a deceased wife's sister to the widower. No strict rules of avoidance existed.

Political organization was as rudimentary as social organization. There were no chiefs or councils. Since the old men of the various local groups had from long experience gained a great knowledge of the area, there developed a passive dominance of the aged. The Medicine man or shaman was probably the most influential individual in this culture. The tenuous nature of subsistence provided for elaboration of hunting magic and a dependence on individual and group rapport with the supernatural.

Religious Patterns

Religious patterns included a belief in a vaguely defined Great Spirit who was the fountainhead of all power but who did not interfere in human affairs. This power could be obtained by men through dreams in which a supernatural patron or guardian spirit endowed the petitioner with a certain amount of power and various songs and procedures needed by the recipient to manipulate his Medicine. There was not much transfer of Medicine from individual to individual. Medicine men worked generally in a benevolent manner and received a small fee for their services. There was also a lively ghost fear and a poorly developed notion of the afterlife.

These people were without war patterns before the advent of the horse. They were raided continually by their more warlike neighbors, but they did not develop an institutionalized form of resistance.

Each local group operated in a specific hunting territory, but there were no notions of land ownership and trespassing was not punished. Their dwellings were crude, temporary brush constructions for the most part. Material possessions were also limited in complexity and amount by the rigors of the environment and the difficulties of transportation. Though the dog was present, it was not used for transportation. A family's possessions were usually carried by the women during the march. Women occupied an inferior position in the society, though they were respected for their full share in the food quest.

A Basin-Type Culture

A Basin-type culture, such as has been briefly described and which could be represented by the historic Wind River Shoshone, was the basic stock from which the Comanche sprang after acquisition of the horse and their subsequent movement onto the Plains. It is probable that these Basin people, living on the western fringes of the Plains, made periodic pedestrian hunting expeditions onto the Plains after buffalo or that they were made aware of the desirable qualities of the buffalo from contact with groups which more thoroughly exploited this beast. Shimkin (Trenholm and Cole 1964:17) suggests that the Shoshone may have roamed the Plains area many generations before finally being driven back into the shelter of the Rockies. Therefore, the Comanche advent can be seen as the appearance on the Plains of a mounted Shoshonean people. The Comanche, with the horse and therefore the ability to efficiently exploit the buffalo herds and the Plains environment, built upon culture patterns already sufficient for this type of life style—exaggerating some, modifying some, deleting others, and developing still others.

On the Plains

With these Plains nomads the laurels went to the young and the physically able, while the older people, valued for their wisdom in Shoshone society, faced an old age of declining social prestige and humiliation. And, though the Comanche lacked a pervasive political organization, the war chief, no longer the Medicine man, became the individual who could wield the most power over the most people at any one time. His authority, however, was temporary and transitory. An elderly man, if he was fortunate, could become a peace chief, but a peace chief possessed no real authority and functioned most importantly as a mediator in the disputes which arose among the younger men.

With the greater food supply offered by the seemingly boundless bison herds, hunting magic decreased in importance. Antelope magic did persist from the Shoshone heritage. The more favorable living conditions and constant food supply also allowed the individual bands, which had retained their Basin characteristics, to become larger and to achieve a greater degree of independence from their sister bands. The emphasis on the buffalo as a food source also tended to decrease the importance of gathering and exploitation of the floral environment for food. Further, the Comanches made little or no use of fish and of such small game as rabbits (Lowie 1954:6).

The Basin Shoshone practice of infanticide disappeared as the family group could more efficiently care for its offspring. The practice of enculturating slaves and captives became common among the Comanches in order to augment their numbers and specifically to free males for hunting and warfare. The stress on war and hunting also tended to debase the position of women, and such practices as the mutilation of wives, a custom which had never occurred in Basin Shoshone culture, came into practice.

Patterns of religious belief and behavior also underwent certain changes from Basin life to the Plains. A vaguely defined belief in a Great Spirit persisted, as did the relative lack of concern with the afterlife. However, the intense fear of ghosts held by the Basin Shoshone diminished in the Comanche Plains culture. Also, the practice of power transmission from individual to individual, instead of power source to individual, developed in importance. The decrease in ghost fear and, it is assumed, witchcraft in Comanche culture, as opposed to the Basin culture, was greatly facilitated by the lessening of intrasocial tensions and the Comanches' ability, through warfare, to turn aggressions outward and away from the primary group. As a whole, Comanche religious patterns were exceedingly simple and lacking in elaborate ceremonialism and ritual, at least compared to their Plains neighbors (Hoebel 1940:83).

The Comanches possessed characteristics, other than their paucity of ceremonialism, which served to differentiate them from other Plains tribes. The Comanche bands were more self-managing than bands found among other Plains groups. Warrior societies, a diagnostic trait of Plains culture, were lacking in Comanche society except in the most rudimentary form. The Sun Dance was not a vital aspect of Comanche culture. Decoration of clothing with beads, quills, and ornaments of bone, shell, and metal was deemphasized, while heavy fringing of the garments was the rule. The Comanche tepee was built on a four-pole base like that of the Blackfoot, Sarsi, Ute, and Shoshone; while the Comanches' historic neighbors, such as the Kiowa, Cheyenne, Arapaho, and Kiowa-Apache used a three-pole foundation (Lowie 1954:33).

By the early nineteenth century the bison herds were greatly diminished on the south Plains, and the Comanches increasingly turned to raiding to augment their economy. During this period the Comanches raided New Mexico, the Santa Fe Trail, northern Texas, and Old Mexico, sometimes as far south as Durango.

Their greatest source of irritation during this span of time was the growing white settlements of Texas. It was during this period of increased contact with Texas that the divisions of the Comanche bands into northern, middle, western, and southern began to acquire a new meaning—one couched in terms of degree of acculturation and the hostilities engendered between the tradition-oriented and conservative Comanche bands and the well-acculturated Comanche bands.

As early as 1779 Governor Don Juan Bautista de Anza of New Spain had recognized the highly independent band organization of Comanche society. The term "tribe" had no political significance for the Comanches. Comanche society consisted of a number of independent and sometimes hostile bands which were linked by only the awareness that they were all *nɜmɜnə*, or "The People." Each band exploited a vaguely defined range within the Comanche country and, with the notable exception of the "Quick Stinger" band, never made war on other bands. There were no pervasive political institutions among the Comanche to mold the bands into a political unit. No tribal council, no joint economic activity, and no ceremonial occasion existed that could unite all the bands for even a brief period of time. The various bands even dealt separately with the United States government. The first and last time that a majority of the bands came together was for the occassion of the first Comanche Sun Dance in 1874, held in the dying moments of the old, free nomadic Comanche culture. This first attempt to organize as a tribe, unfortunately for the Comanches, was attempted too late, for by this time the end of the nomadic Comanche life way was but a year in the future.

The Spanish government of New Spain considered the Comanches as being organized into three major bands. The Anglo-Americans also designated three divisions—northern, middle, and southern. Wallace and Hoebel (1925:25) record that Robert S. Neighbors, in 1860, cited the existence of eight Comanche bands; James Mooney later listed thirteen; Robert Lowie in 1912 mentioned only four. The Santa Fe Laboratory group in 1933 was able to gain information concerning thirteen bands. I was able to find evidence of five Comanche bands— *yapai* ("Root Eaters"), *kwahada* ("Antelopes"), *hɔnitaiβ* ("Corn White Men"); or *pɛnatɜkə* ("Eating Honey All the Time"), *honono* ("Hill People"), and *noyaka* or *nokoni* ("Always Moving Around").

Comanche Bands

There is no information on the origins of the various bands or their pre-contact composition and geographical placement. In the following discussion of the major Comanche bands the reconstructed situation is that of the Comanche in their historic territory from approximately the late eighteenth century until the disintegration of the old nomadic Comanche culture in the latter part of the nineteenth century.

The largest Comanche band was the *pɛnatɜkə*, or "Honey Eaters," the southernmost Comanche band. At various times they were known as the "Hospitables," "No Meat," "Steep Climbers," "Wasps" or "Quick Stingers," and "Timber People." This band was the vanguard of the Comanches' southward migration.

The final territory they held was northcentral Texas. Early references by Anglo-Americans concerning the Comanches pertain mainly to these people. Wallace and Hoebel (1952:25) mention that they lived near the white settlements and associated more with the Caddos, Wichitas, and whites in historic times than with their western and northern kinsmen. Both their tradition and that of the northern Comanche bands tell how the two lost contact for a long period of time. It was only with the northern Comanches' raids into Mexico that the two groups finally reestablished ties.

The *penatʒkə* were put on reservations in Texas in 1854, while the majority of Comanches continued to raid freely throughout Texas. The reservation experiment failed, largely because of pressure from the white citizenry, and was ended in 1858. By this time the power of the Honey Eaters was minimal and, because of their proximity to the Texas settlements, they were made to suffer for many of the crimes perpetrated by the "wild" western and northern Comanches.

The *nɔkoni*, "Those Who Move Often," was the major band representing the middle Comanches. The center of their range was the Pease River region of Texas. The *tanima*, "Liver Eaters," and *kutsuɛka*, "Buffalo Eaters," composed the remaining middle Comanche bands, sharing the range of the *nɔkoni*.

The *kwahada*, "Antelope" band, is the representative of the western Comanches. They probably drifted south at approximately the same time as the *yapai* band and later moved onto the staked Plains. In late historic times the *kwahada* band was the most warlike of the Comanches and the last band to surrender to the United States Army.

The *yapai*, or *Yamparika*, "Yap Eaters," occupied the northernmost reaches of the Comanche country. The *yapai* was probably the last band to break from the Shoshonean traditions. Wallace and Hoebel (1952:27) write that the Fort Hall Shoshone of Idaho call all Comanches *Yamparika*. During the late nineteenth century they were situated from the south side of the Arkansas River to the Canadian River.

Acculturation and Schism

The reservation and postreservation period wrought great changes in the function and composition of the Comanche bands. Matters of protection, subsistence, and territory were taken from the control of the Comanches and brought under the power of various agencies of, or appointed by, the federal government. It was only with the land allotments of the Jerome Act in 1901 and 1905 that the members of the various bands were able to assert their band identity once again in real estate. Today, in Comanche, Cotton, and Caddo counties, the ancient geographic distribution of the four major bands is stated in miniature. The *yapai* are still the northernmost band, centered in the area delimited by the Oklahoma communities of Medicine Park, Meers, Elgin, Fletcher, Cyril, Apache, and Bonne. The *nɔkoni* are located south of the *yapai* and north of Lawton, Oklahoma. The greatest density of *kwahada* population is in western Comanche County in the towns of Cache, Snyder, and Indiahoma. The *pɛnatɔkɔ* continue to be the southern-most of the Comanche bands, centered in the vicinity of Walters, Oklahoma.

Perhaps the most ubiquitous and pervasive problems which have confronted the Comanche in the twentieth century are those directly associated with the process of acculturation with the dominant white culture. The traditional–progressive and conservative–liberal schism which has appeared as a disruptive force in contemporary Comanche society very closely follows band boundaries. As might be expected, the southern band, the *pɛnatɔkɔ*, a people with a relatively long history of white contact experience, have been more successful in their transition into the twentieth century than have the *yapai* Comanches, the band with the least amount of contact experience. At present the *pɛnatɔkɔ* are the progressive and liberal Comanches, while the *yapai* stand as the rallying point for all traditionally oriented and conservative Comanches. The *yapai* are joined in the traditionalist camp by the *kwahada* and the *nɔkoni*. This major division is thought of by the Comanches as a division between the northern "tribes" and the southern "tribes."

Most contemporary northern Comanches do not use the term *pɛnatɔkɔ* for the southern people; rather they call them *hɔnitaiβo*, which means "eat corn like a white man," or, more literally, "corn white men." They are often referred to in English as "Freckles," alluding to the great degree of mixed-blood Comanches who, the northerners believe, fill the southerner's ranks. The southern Comanches are less colorful than the northerners in their invectives, simply stating that the northerners are, for the most part, uneducated, drunken, shiftless, and generally responsible for the poor reputation which the Comanches possess in many of the white communities in southern Oklahoma.

Historical indications of the basis for the present-day dichotomy of Comanche society are suggested by Richardson in *The Comanche Barrier to South Plains Settlement* (1933). Perhaps the most significant single factor responsible for the subsequent divisiveness of the northern and southern Comanche bands is the geographic distance which separated them well into historic times. At the peak of Comanche territorial expansion, as many as 600 miles could have separated the northern bands, ranging in southern Colorado and southwestern Kansas, from southern bands, inhabiting northcentral Texas.

The Kiowa and northern Comanches made a treaty in 1790 which did not include the southern Comanche bands. This treaty was never broken. During the Texas Revolution the southern bands refrained from taking advantage of the chaos in Texas to raid and plunder, while the northern Comanches and their Kiowa allies joined to make one of the most destructive Indian raids in Texas history. After the Mexican defeat in 1837 the Cherokee chief, Bowl, was commissioned to visit the various Comanche bands to seek peace. The southerners were cooperative and friendly; the northerners, however, were insulting and hostile. In the 1850s when the southern bands were put on reservations in Texas, the northern bands continued their raiding activities with the Kiowas. During this time agent officials complained of the demoralizing effects which the northern Comanches had on the southern reservation wards. Further, members of the southern (Wasps or Quick Stingers) band joined the United States Army in its war against the "wild" northern Comanche bands. This bit of "Freckle" treachery is still perpetuated in the war stories told by the northerners.

The most obvious contemporary example of the ancient roots of this Comanche factionalism concerns the Kiowa-Comanche-Apache constitution established as a result of the Medicine Lodge Treaty of 1867. The southerners favor a separate Comanche constitution, while the northerners view this as an attempt to break the long-standing alliance between the northern Comanches and the Kiowas. Sanapia's statement on this subject is typical of the northerner's sentiment.

> Here, up to today, those Walter's people are trying to break us up. How could they do that? I got grandchildren that's Kiowa, and the Comanches are all mixed in with them Kiowas. We all together . . . got to stay that way. Those southern people aren't like us. All their old people are Mexicans. Well, they Comanches, same as us, but they act like white people. We've been with these Kiowas and Apaches for a long time, and we can't break it up.

Of course, this traditional–progressive and conservative–liberal differentiation suggests but the grossest divisions in Comanche society. There is also the Christian–peyotist factionalism, for example; however, like the other minor factional elements, it is subsumed under the greater northern–southern Comanche divisions. The northern people consider themselves peyotist and look with scorn on the southerner's predilection for Christianity—the white man's religion. The southerners consider the northerners' religious bias primitive and heathenish and but a further example of the inferiority of the northerners in general. In my field research I found the southern Comanches, relative to the northern Comanches, to be generally lacking in knowledge of, or sympathy toward, those aspects of Comanche culture considered by the northerners and Comanche literature to be traditional in nature, that is, relating to the time of the nomadic culture of the Comanches and the values and world view which it posited.

The preceding account of northern versus southern Comanche orientation is intended as a generalizing descriptive attempt. There are, of course, progressive northern Comanches and conservative southern Comanches. However, the relatively rigidly defined spatial distribution of the opposing "tribes" will usually call for the progressively oriented northerner to move south and the conservative southerner to move north. I observed several instances in which an individual, in order to visibly state his factional allegiance, moved his abode into the geographic area most closely identified with the faction which he supported.

Sanapia is a *yapai* Comanche and an archconservative and traditionalist. The majority of my informants were also northern Comanches, though not all were *yapai*. These were the only people who possessed some "accurate" knowledge concerning native doctors and doctoring practices and who actually interacted in this institutionalized framework. The southerners, recognizing Sanapia's role among the northerners, emphasized the superiority of white doctors over the "superstitious" doctoring practices valued by the majority of northerners.

2

Sanapia, 1895–1968

Early Childhood

SANAPIA WAS BORN at Fort Sill, Oklahoma, in the spring of 1895 in a tcpcc encampment of *yapai* Comanches who had traveled to Fort Sill for rations from the vicinity of Medicine Park, Oklahoma. As with most Comanche women her age, Sanapia only knows that she was born in the spring and has therefore arbitrarily set her birth date at May twentieth.

Her father was Comanche and her mother Comanche-Arapaho. Sanapia was the sixth in a family of eleven siblings, having five older brothers, three younger brothers, and two younger sisters. As is still the custom among the more traditionally oriented Comanches, the maternal grandmother is very instrumental in rearing her daughter's children. Both Sanapia's mother and her mother's older brother were eagle doctors.

> Yeah, my mother doctored . . . she could do anything. One time it was her playmate . . . one time they were playing and she died. They put her buckskin dress on her, and you know in them days when anybody died they put red paint all over their face and their arms and their feet and then they put them away. They fix her up like that. My mother was playing with the rest of the kids. She was just a little bitty girl. She said, "I'm going to my tent and go to sleep. After awhile I play some more." Later these kids came to her and said, "They want you over there. Go to doctor." And she was just about ten years old that time. She went down there and she said, "No, no, she not going to go. I don't want her to die. I'll fix her up." She told all those people that, "You all get out. I'll fix her up." And she was sitting in that tent making all kinds of racket and pretty soon that little girl get up. She came back to life and lived many years. My mother died before her.

Sanapia's maternal uncle was also very active among Comanche peyotists, leading peyote meetings throughout southern Oklahoma. Sanapia also counts among her relatives a paternal grandfather who was an important *yapai* leader in the late nineteenth century and another maternal uncle who was a twentieth-century Arapaho chief. Each of these facts is individually significant for an understanding of some of the major early influences which affected Sanapia's life.

The recurring descriptive phrase used by my older Comanche informants when speaking of Sanapia's father was, "He was a strong Christian man." His conversion to Christianity occurred in his early middle years, shortly before Sanapia's birth; and, in fact, it was the Presbyterian minister responsible for the father's conversion who was given the honor of naming the new born Sanapia. Her father devoted most of his life to Christian activities among the Comanches, much to the later embarrassment of Sanapia. He was also energetic in attempting to learn and to incorporate into his family's routine the life style of white society. Sanapia's reminiscences of her father depend for their tone and complexion on her vacillating moods. At one time she may speak of him as "a good Christian man and a good father," and at another time she might speak of a father who, through his white-Christian–modeled behavior, brought ridicule upon his wife and family from the Comanche community in which they lived.

You know, he was the first Christian man among us Comanche peoples. He used to go up to Richard Spur and talk to them people up there. He talk about the bible and things like that. And you know, some of those Indians believed him, what he tells them, but some of them make fun of him and tell him that he don't know nothing about the bible, or he don't know nothing about white

Sanapia and her parents, 1898.

Yapai Comanche band "chief" in 1890. Sanapia's maternal grandfather.

man's ways. They say, "We don't want to hear stories about white people that been dead for years . . . dead for a long time." That's what they tell him. When he prayed, some of those people, they tell him, "Who you praying to?" And he said, "Well, I pray to God because the white man told me to." And they just laugh at him. He catch them when they out of peyote meeting on Sunday mornings. Maybe he shouldn't have done that. You wouldn't catch my mother going over there with him. No!

When Sanapia's father embraced Christianity, he turned totally from all things Comanche; at least, this is the opinion of those who knew him. A photograph of his wife and him taken in the early twentieth century shows a massive man with short hair, stiffly posing, dressed in a dark suit, dark shoes, white shirt, starched collar, and tie. Beside him stands his wife, dressed in the cloth "squaw dress," apron, sash, and buckskin moccasins, a costume commonly worn by women in the immedite postreservation period, but displaying in her attire style not one trace of the effects of the surrounding white society. This photograph dramatically

Sanapia's maternal uncle.

conveys the nature of a very far-reaching influence on Sanapia's life: a liberal father who attempted to incorporate into his person visible symbols of the white-Christian culture in which he found himself enveloped and an extremely conservative and traditionally oriented mother who had nothing but disdain for the symbols and values of white society.

Sanapia's mother seems to have been almost fanatical in her conservatism. For example, though she knew and understood English, she would never speak it in a white man's presence, feeling that somehow this would belittle her in the

Sanapia's mother and father.

Sanapia's mother, 1909.

white man's eyes. Sanapia remembers this point well, for it was she, as her mother's favorite daughter, who was called upon to take her mother to the nearby towns and act as interpreter.

Lots of times I would be playing or something and I have to go with her . . . speak for her. I tell her, "You can talk English good, why do I have to talk for you?" She just tell me to come on. She said that when the white mans learn Comanche talk, she would learn white man language. She was real stubborn, I guess you would say, about things like that. You know, one time my father put these little napkin rings like they used at school on our table and he told us kids to use them. Well, my mother got them and put bead work on them with each our name on each one. My father got mad at that, but my mother told him that she wasn't no white man, she was Indian. They would talk like that a lot but they stay together till they both dead. They have some run-ins though. Like once I come back from school with these button-top shoes. My mother made me take them off because she said they would cripple my feet. My grandmother told me that too. But my father liked them and made me wear them. I thought they looked good, you know, but they hurt if you wear them long enough. I go barefoot a lot when I was a real young woman.

According to Sanapia's memory, her father never took issue with the mother's doctoring activities or her involvement with the peyotists. From Sanapia's stories of childhood it seems that it was the mother who would react violently against the father's attempt to introduce elements of white culture into the home. The father apparently never directly attacked the conservative Comanche ways but preferred to ignore them, withdraw from them, or illustrate how the white man's "road" was superior.

Sanapia's memories of her maternal grandmother are the fondest and most elaborated. It was this grandmother who took the greatest hand in rearing the children, though the father and mother acted as final authorities. It was also this grandmother who continually emphasized to Sanapia the importance of remembering the old ways and old stories, even suggesting that she keep a diary or journal of her life.

My grandmother was just a little bitty woman. She stayed in her tepee south of the house because she didn't like houses. She said that they good for keeping dogs and horses and that's all. A lot of old peoples would used to joke like that. She sure was good to me . . . take care of me all the time when I was just a small girl. She wrap me in her blanket when I was little, even when I get to be five years old . . . pretty big girl by then . . . and she carry me around. She said, "I want you to save your feet, don't let your legs get tired because you got a long time to live." She carry me around down on the creek, doing nothing, until I get tired and then she take me back to her tent. She rocks me to sleep and if I wake up way in the night, she would give me a meat ball . . . pound meat with sugar on it. Then she poke up the fire and tell me old stories. She told me how to make real old time Indian bags out of this softest buckskin so I could carry around my own little meat balls in there. Bag looks like a flat bag sort of is the kind of one I had. She tell me always to remember what she tells me and I did. She tell me that I should write it down, but at that time I didn't even know what writing is, but my grandma did. She tell me that a lot of white people would come into our country. That was even before I seen a lot of white people like now. I remember that when I was small I watched long bunch of white peoples come in here and up to today that's almost all there is around here. In them days, no fences and no white people. And my grandmother knew that before it happened. She know lot of things like that too. And when what she says happens I was sure surprised, but it made me believe her better. She had a big hunk out of her ear. She cut her ear up when her brother died in the war . . . to show how sorry she was, but I didn't know that and I would joke her and tell her, "What's the matter with your ear? Did a mule bite it off?" She would tell me what happened to it. I would ask her all sorts of things and she would always tell me something on it. She's the one who told me to take my mother's doctoring-way when I was getting older. I didn't want it because I thought it was silly or nasty, but my grandmother said that soon in the future there wouldn't be hardly any Indian doctors left and she sure was right on that. I really cried when she pass on, because she had been so good to me, bringing me along like she did. So now, up to today, my daughters got kids and my son. I try to be like my grandma. I tell them old ways that I can remember, but, you know, they don't hardly care for it. They getting to be more like white peoples every year that pass. My grandmother told me all this would happen too.

Sanapia's maternal uncle, an eagle doctor like her mother, was very active among peyotists in southern Oklahoma. Her first recollections of peyote meetings were those which were directed by her uncle, and it was through him that Sanapia later learned the manifold uses of peyote as a medicine. Her mother also utilized peyote as a medicine, though not to the extent to which her uncle employed it. Sanapia's paternal grandfather was also a "strong peyote man." Thus early in life Sanapia was impressed with the importance of peyote by two very influential family members.

Religious Influences

Sanapia was reared in an atmosphere colored by three basic approaches to supernaturalistic realms—the Christianity of her father, the peyotism of her uncle and paternal grandfather, and the more customary Plains pattern of vision quests and guardian spirits as embodied by her mother, the eagle doctor. Through this liberal education she learned the basic tenets of each and managed to syncretically combine elements of all three into the validating and supportive unity by which she now lives and finds the rationalization for her own supernatural prerogative as a Medicine woman.

She quite naturally deemphasizes the differences and emphasizes the similarities in these three supernaturalistic systems. She is very fond of making comments like the following:

You know, the bible says that when Jesus was on earth he would heal people. His disciples had that same power as Him, and I know I'm just like them. I got power in my hands to heal peoples too. You can read the bible to find out that Jesus gives those people power to help people that got sickness, and it's just like that with me. When I pray, I feel just like, well, the Lord says, "You go heal that person. I give you power to do that and give you a good mind . . . put power in your hands. When you touch anybody like that, you'll get them well." That's what I always thought, you know. Use the bible like that.

She speaks similarly of peyote:

That peyote is a real good medicine. They call it . . . some of the Indians call it a sacrament like white peoples who are Christians. God gave that peyote to the Indians to help them when they got sickness. I learned how to use that peyote a lot of ways. You ain't supposed to take it and think you go crazy. No! It's a medicine and that's the way I use it. Peyote gives me power to make people well.

When speaking of her supernatural patron, the eagle, she says:

The eagle got more power then anything living, I guess. Its got Medicine to help people get well . . . to cure them. I got power like that eagle because the eagle help me when I call on it when I doctor. My mother told me that I be just like that eagle when I doctor. I can feel the eagle working in me when I doctor and try hard to get somebody well. Feels like that eagle tell me in my mind to go ahead and fix that person up . . . get him well.

However, though she utilizes elements of peyotism and Christianity, she has little sympathy for the organized forms of these religions. This is especially true with regard to Christianity.

The way I know is, when I went to Christian church up there, many, many years back I found out some things. Like when you get hard up, or when you get sick in the family, they ain't going to help you. They don't come. They don't say, "Let's have a prayer meeting for you. Let's do that." They don't say that to you. They really tight. They don't spare nothing with you. I still pray like that, but I'm not going to their church for nothing.

She speaks of the Native American Church:

They say I supposed to sign my name to belong to that Native Church. I told them that I wasn't going to do that. I been using that medicine for long as I know it, and my mother before me, and her father before her and way, way back like that. I don't have to belong to nothing to use that medicine. We hold meetings here on our place but I ain't going nowhere else around here to peyote meeting. That medicine belong to anybody that needs it and you don't have to belong to the church that they set up if you want to use it.

White Contact

Sanapia's first extensive contact with white society came when she began her schooling at the age of seven at Cache Creek Mission School in southern Oklahoma. She remembers the seven years she spent at Cache Creek as generally pleasant.

I really did enjoy that school. I like it. The teachers . . . every one of them and our superintendent were all missionaries. They were really nice people. They teach us the bible. All the girls and boys go up there and they teach us all these bible stories and they question us out of the bible to see if we really read it.

They teach us the men. We all sitting around there. When she tell us how Jesus was born, we just laugh and act silly and our matron would say, "Don't laugh." Then we ask her, "Did you see the baby?" You know, things like that . . . the older girls and us ask her questions like that. We just laugh about it. All the time we thought it was silly for them not to go and see the baby when it was born. Yeah, we learn how to write and learn how to spell, and arithmetic and whatever they learn us. We caught onto it. Then the government wrote a letter to our superintendent and said to send a bunch of them to Haskell in Kansas. And they sent a bunch of them over there and they went to school up there for about three years and they come back and they were grown and they all got married, but I didn't go. My mother wouldn't sign the papers and my dad wouldn't let me go. "No, we don't want her to go up there. She might run off or she'll freeze to death or somebody might kill her on the road." So a bunch of us girls, we didn't go. And a bunch of them went. My brothers went. They were younger than I and they went. And my mother said, "No, she's not going, but you boys could go. Boys are tougher than the girls." That what she told my brothers and so they went. I didn't care nothing about it either way.

During the summer vacations she would return to her home, which at that time was situated along Chandler Creek in Comanche County, Oklahoma.

I never did go places because we didn't have no places to go in them days . . . no cars or nothing. When we come out of school we just stay home all summer. Help my father with the work and everything he's got. He had lots of crops. My brothers cultivate that corn. I have to ride the horse for them and keep it on the row because the corn was so high that the horse would keep eating back and forth and my father would make me ride that horse to keep him on that line so he won't be eating the tops of the corn. They take turns, three of my brothers, while I be riding that horse all day, all day. In the morning we go plow till noon and then we go to dinner and then we go back and plow again till we get through with it. My father used to teach us to work, you know.

It was during summer vacation prior to her last year at school that Sanapia's mother offered to train her to become a doctor. Sanapia was reticent at first, but combined pressure from her mother and maternal grandmother persuaded her to at least consent to the first phases of this training program, that of learning to identify in their natural habitat the various floral medicines which her mother used in doctoring.

The Middle Years

Sanapia left school when she was fourteen years old, and her activities for the next three years were in the main involved with the training program her mother and uncle had established to teach Sanapia all she would need to know to become an eagle doctor. By her seventeenth year Sanapia had successfully completed her training and possessed all the skills, knowledge, and supernatural powers which she would employ in doctoring after she passed menopause. During the period of training her mother had dissuaded her from marriage so that she would be able to give her full attention to learning the skills of the eagle doctor. Much of this dissuasive effort was also aimed at Sanapia's older brother since it was the brother who had the prerogative of giving his sister away in marriage. However, after her training both the mother and the older brother immediately joined in a combined effort to find Sanapia a good husband.

Sanapia, age 16 (left) and her young sister (right). Taken in Lawton, Oklahoma, 1912.

Well, my brother was chumming around with this young boy. He was about nineteen and he went to Fort Sill School. And my brother, he go down there and come home with him sometimes. Finally, that summer when school was out, he brought that young man home with him and he stayed with us all summer. My mother said, "You better get married to this boy. He's a nice boy. He always helping with everything, and he might work for us if you get married to him." I didn't have no sense enough to . . . I mean I don't think about love, or anything like that. So I said, "If he wants to marry me, I marry him." So my mother said, "Do you want to marry my daughter?" and he said, "Yeah, I'll marry her." And that's the way I got married. They just give their kids away like that. If you ask anybody, "Do you want to marry my daughter?" They say, "Yeah." That's your husband . . . just like that.

Sanapia had one son, and shortly after his birth she left her first husband at the urging of her mother. She married again within a year and remained married to her second husband until his death in the early 1930s. She had a son and a daughter by her second husband. Following the death of her second husband, Sanapia's life took on a tone which is recalled most vividly by those who wish to discredit her. During this time her violent bursts of temper, excessive drinking, sexual promiscuity, and zest for gambling won for her a notoriety which has never entirely left her. She talks of those years as "the time I was roughing it out."

Sanapia's second husband was apparently her favorite. He is also the only one of her spouses which she refers to as "husband." She was emotionally very ravaged by his death. It is interesting that the more tradition-oriented informants will mention Sanapia's misbehavior after his death but add no note of blame, simply emphasizing her grief. Kardiner (1945:77) makes the following statement, when discussing a Comanche woman's behavior after the death of her child. Perhaps the reaction to the death of a loved husband could correspond to the same pattern.

After the death of a child a young woman who had previously been entirely respectable would become exceedingly active sexually and would have a whole series of affairs. This behavior, which sometimes lasted two or three years, was recognized as a sort of psychotic state and did not result in the same sort of difficulties that accompanied elopement or break-up of a marriage. The husband would feel sorry and would wait until she recovered and then resume the regular marriage relationship.

It was during the years when Sanapia was "roughing it out" that she first attempted to employ her doctoring skills. She was approached by a sister who wished Sanapia to doctor her sick child.

She came to visit me one day when I was around here. She rolled a smoke with that Bull Durham and handed it to me, and I took it. I didn't even think what she was here for, but then I knew. She ask me to doctor her sick baby. I got so nervous I just start to shake all over and I told her to go away because I was feeling shame, I guess. Then I start to think what my mother told me, how I couldn't refuse nobody, so I went with her. I kept thinking that I couldn't do no good, but you know, I got that baby well. I thought that was some kind of sign, so I thought that I might try to make something out of this doctoring.

Some years later Sanapia married again, and many of my informants say that it was at this time that Sanapia abruptly ceased the behavior which had caused her so much notoriety. This was also the period during which Sanapia earnestly began her career as a doctor. Every account of cases which Sanapia treated stems from a time no later than 1945.

Sanapia and her present spouse have traveled extensively in the western United States. Their route always corresponds to areas of Indian population density. In the following, Sanapia recounts her first excursion to Wyoming.

We went to New Mexico and to Las Vegas. We went over there. We just went, you know. We don't know where we going but we just went that way. Came to Navajos, Pueblos, and we visit among them and we stop at Las Vegas. Mind you, at that time I sure like to gamble. And so I went over there and start gambling. J———— [Sanapia's husband] said, "You better quit. We long way from home." And I just said, "As long as we stay here I'm going to gamble. If we lose anything, I win it back." Wanted him to get me some money. And so we stayed about ten days and then we went on. We went to Wyoming. They, the Shoshones, live in a reservation at Fort Washington, north from Lander, . . . town of that name, I think. Maybe something else. They live close together to one another, you know, not like us. We live so many miles from each other. They don't work, they don't do nothing. Just all day long they drum and sing and dance and every day something is going on and gambling is the biggest part of it. Well, when we first got over to Wyoming, that afternoon, we ask where are the Shoshone peoples. We was right there among them and we didn't even know it. We went into a big building, you know . . . it was their community building or something like a club or something like that. We went in. It was full of Indians. They was sitting around in groups around the floor. And there was blankets and they was sitting on it. And then we stand there and look at them and they was gambling . . . playing Mexican monte. And so I wanted to find out what my grandmather had told me so I went up and listen and when they talk about us. We didn't talk. We just standing there. And they said "These are some kind of Indians, maybe Mexicans. They sure look like Mexicans." They said that. And we said, "We not Mexicans," . . . in Indian. And they look at one another and said, "Do you all talk like us?" and we said, "Yeah, we talk like you all." I said, "We your ancestors. That where we come from." So that evening they invite us to their homes . . . this whole group of people and that night we have group of Indians there. They were all talking to us . . . finding out where we live and where we come from and all that. And I told them, "You are the people that my grandmother told me about." And I told them about that big sickness what the Indians caught, and then I said, "You all got that and then you scattered. You belong to our tribe. That's what my grandmother told me." And they were surprised, you know.

Training to Become a Doctor

Sanapia recalls the four years of training to become a doctor as the most important years of her life. It is to those years that Sanapia owes the prestige which she enjoys today among the northern Comanches. As a doctor, she holds a status in her society equal to a man. She is at the zenith of traditionally defined prestige and social power acquirable by a woman in Comanche society.

The first phase of Sanapia's training began in the summer before her last year of school. This first phase consisted of lessons in identifying certain medicine plants in the field and in the avenues of acquisition of medicines which were not native to southern Oklahoma. Sanapia was also taught the rituals involved in the collection of certain plants and the various manners of rendering raw plant parts into manipulatable medicine. Concomitantly, she was instructed in the skills of administering medicines.

The first phase initiated Sanapia's training period and continued throughout the next three years. Sanapia was next instructed in the diagnosing of all manner of human afflictions and their proper treatment. During this time she served as an aid to her mother and maternal uncle in their doctoring activities and thus was able to observe the actual treatment of patients as well as the required deportment of a doctor and his patient. However, knowledge of ethics and required role behavior of a doctor was not left to Sanapia's youthful observations alone. She remembers "long, long talks" when her mother and uncle would impress on her the proper behavior of a doctor.

These rules of conduct, in the way in which they deemphasize the significance of the individual and emphasize the supernatural powers operating through him, seem to have a distinctly Judao-Christian cast to them and appear to be somewhat counter to the more individual-oriented supernaturalistic notions recorded for the Comanches of an earlier time. Perhaps Sanapia, in her attempt to construct a unified religious structure from the three disparate supernaturalistic systems into which she was born, has slightly modified the tenor of the eagle doctor ethics and their premises, as taught by her mother and maternal uncle, to make them more compatible with other elements in her own personal syncretic supernaturalistic complex. It is highly doubtful that her mother, with her aversion to Christianity, would have so sensitively and systematically performed this feat.

Deportment of a Doctor

Most importantly, the doctor must lead a good and honorable life. The Medicine demands this, and it would do harm to the individual possessing it if he acted in a manner unbecoming a *puhakut*. Sanapia suggests that a *puhakut* and his Medicine are one. If a possessor of power, through his untoward behavior, brings disgrace on himself, he also brings disgrace on his Medicine, and as punishment his power could cause his death.

The doctor must also be always accessible. He cannot refuse anyone his services. Sanapia conceptualizes herself, in the role of eagle doctor, as the medium through which the Medicine operates. She "possesses" Medicine only in this sense, and, once she has committed herself to the life of a *puhakut*, it is no longer her decision as to who may or may not benefit from a supernatural power acting through her which can alleviate human suffering.

An eagle doctor must never extol his own abilities and should also dissuade others from doing so. Once again, Sanapia interprets this as a further means by which the doctor recognizes that it is not the doctor but the Medicine with which he has been gifted, which is responsible for the good works which are accomplished by him.

A doctor should never suggest that he could cure an individual but must wait for the individual to approach him. Again Sanapia states that a violation of this norm would be an indication on the part of the doctor that he, and only secondarily his Medicine, is the important element in the potential curing.

A doctor must be paid for any services he renders, no matter how slight. Similarly, a doctor cannot work his Medicine without payment. In the case of an eagle doctor, this applies even to family members. In addition, the payment, with the exception of certain relatively inexpensive ritual items (green cloth and tobacco) required at the first interview of doctor and patient, must be left to the discretion of the patient. A doctor cannot refuse anything which is offered in payment. Furthermore, Sanapia was instructed that she must immediately give away a portion of her final payment to anyone in her immediate vicinity at the time of payment. This "give away" is a means by which Sanapia honors her Medicine.

And one thing, when they come to me . . . anybody comes to me and say, "I want you to doctor me," bring plain goods, no figure or nothing. Dark green goods. They have to take that and smoke and they going to give me that green goods. Either a yard or two or three or four yards like that. That's the only thing I ask for. And they say, "Now what else we going to pay you when you get this boy, this girl, this woman, this man well?" I say, "That's what I call for . . . just the green goods. And if he gets well or she gets well, its up to you. If you think I get that person well, its up to you." But I'm not going to say I want this and that and that and I want so much money. I'm not going to say that because that's what my mother told me. She said, "Don't you ever ask for anything. Its going to be given to you. I don't care what anybody says, its going to come to you." Now, up to today, when anybody give to me . . . give me blanket or any kind of goods . . . I ain't supposed to keep it. It be like somebody come here and I doctor them and they get well and they come in and pile things up here for me and those girls are out there. I call them and say, "Here, you all. Take you choice out of this." And whatever they leave, that's mine. And that's the way I get all my things today and that was my mother's words . . . what she told me to do.

Origin of Eagle Doctors

It was also during this period of training that Sanapia was told the origin story of the Comanche eagle doctors.

Way back in years there used to be an old woman who was pretty poor. She had a grandson she tried her best to take care of because all her children were gone and all that was left was this grandson. When them people moved their camps, she used to trail behind them. When they set up another camp, the old woman would camp right outside on the edge of that camp place. Sometimes people, mens, brought them food, meat, you know. But most times they were poor and hungry. And it went on and went on till one time they were all down south and west among them Navajo and Pueblo peoples. They was all trading each other. Meat and blankets for corn and meal and things. One Comanche young man got a whole pile of that corn meal and brought it to the old woman. That's the only way they could get that stuff them days. The grandson was happy over that, you know, over that young man bringing those things and helping them out. Well, later on the grandmother was cooking that corn and her grandson wanted some. The woman said, "No, I can't get any right this minute. I'm too busy to mess with you." Her grandson asked again but he got that same answer. He ask four times until he just fell over backwards and started crying and hollering real loud. Then he told his grandmother that he was going to be an eagle and leave her. Sure enough, he started growing wings on his shoulders. The grandmother thought he was joking, but soon and soon he had wings. When the old woman saw that she start to cry but the boy said, "No, you been stingy and I'm going to go . . . going to leave you all." The grandmother was crying and beggin' him not to go and soon a bunch of people came around her tepee. She ran out and told them what was happening but they didn't do nothing. I guess they thought she was crazy. But then, all at once, the boy came out and flapped his eagle wings and flew up and up. He went over them four times. He told them, "I'm leaving because that old woman was stingy with me." Then he took a feather from his tail and dropped it and it came down real slow, this way and that way, back and forth and back and forth. Then he said, "I'm going to leave you people this thing. Whoever gets that feather when it lands will have my help when ever he or she needs it to help some other people." And don't you know, the first person to get that feather was just a little girl. She was the first one what had that eagle's power like he said.

Consent of the Teachers

During the four years of her training Sanapia was closely observed by four individuals—her mother, maternal uncle, maternal grandmother, and paternal grandfather. Each had to give approval, by means of a blessing ceremony, before Sanapia's mother could complete the last phase of the training, the actual transmission of her supernatural powers. Sanapia's mother could usurp the prerogative of the other three mentors; however, this would be considered a serious breach of etiquette and proper procedure. It would also tend to make Sanapia suspect as a witch since it would be known, by broadcast of the three slighted mentors, that there was no way to know for certain that Sanapia had truly learned to use her powers in the proper manner. Ideally, each of the four individuals would act as Sanapia's adviser and teacher; though it would be the mother and maternal uncle, in Sanapia's case, who would be solely responsible for instruction in the skills of doctoring, while the maternal grandmother and paternal grandfather would dwell upon instilling in her a proper system of values, morals, and ethics.

The notion that supernatural power is potentially dangerous for group welfare will appear repeatedly in the following discussion. This belief seems to be the basis for the four-man "review board" in Sanapia's training. A *puhakut* can do great good for his people, but he is also capable of tremendous evil. By a series of checks by the four advisers, the potential of evil tendencies in a training Medicine possessor can be more readily detected. If the one who will do the actual transmission of power overrides the other three mentors, at least the community can be warned of this; that is, the new *puhakut*, because of his lack of ethical training, may use his powers for evil.

Sanapia's maternal grandmother was the first one to bless her, thus giving her approval to Sanapia's becoming a doctor. The paternal grandfather's blessing ceremony was similar, in its essentials, to the following description given by Sanapia of the blessing by her grandmother:

One morning she told my mother, "This morning I'm going to bless my granddaughter. I want to fix it. I want my son to go out there and build a fire and when it turns to coals he could bring me some." And she had a little iron bucket, you know, and she said, "Put that big coal in this iron and bring it into my tepee. I want to bless her so she could live a long time and help people. And then she going to have children. And whatever she wants, anything at all, she's going to get it . . . easy way . . . she won't have to work, she won't have to do nothing." That's what she said, and then she blessed me. I was pretty good size, about fourteen I guess. She blessed me with all what she said and then she put cedar on them coals and she pray and sing. Then she put her hand on my head and I inhale that cedar and she fan it on my legs and arms, all over my body. She would sing a song and then she prayed some more. And you know, in them days I never did know how they prayed, but she would pray and she said, "You, I don't know what you are, but I want you to bless this little girl so she can grow up and live to be an old lady like me. You, the one who go in the night and watch people, I don't know who you are, but you're like that, bless her. And this earth, I want her to walk on you for many, many years. I want her to be strong and healthy and I want her to live many years." And after she got through, she took that red paint and put water in it and rubbed it like that. Just smeared it all on my face, and rubbed it from my knees down to the bottom of my feet. Then she said, "Now, she's going to stand on this earth. This paint comes from the earth and she's going to stand on it. And she's going to live long life after she gets old. Help peoples. And when she gets real old, and her hair turns gray and white and her teeth fall out, well, that's when she's going to die." That's what she told me.

In the early 1900s a flu epidemic struck the Comanches. Sanapia was afflicted, and her maternal uncle was summoned to treat her. It was during this treatment that the uncle gave his consent by including phrasing in his standard blessing ceremony at the termination of treatment which meant that Sanapia would regain her health only if she would devote her life to the profession of doctoring. Frightened by this bit of "blackmail," Sanapia promised that she would always strive to be a good woman and a good doctor. As a symbol of her promise, the uncle gave her a new name, "Memory Woman," signifying that Sanapia should never forget the oath made to her uncle as a condition for her regained health.

The next to give consent was the grandfather, but the final and most crucial consent needed was that of the mother. It was given early in the last year of training. With the mother's blessing–consent, the actual transfer of power began. This transference of supernatural power from the mother would progress through four stages, culminating in Sanapia's four days and nights of solitary meditation. The four-day ordeal, or vision quest, signals the termination of training, for it is at this time that the neophyte eagle doctor's power is tested during the period of solitary meditation as the ghosts converge on him in an attempt to frighten and harass him to the point that he will renounce his Medicine. In other words, even with the consent of the teacher and the three advisers, the actual fait accompli is ultimately the outcome of a kind of mystical combat between the malevolent spirits of the dead and the Medicine of the potential eagle doctor. Kardiner's (1945:93) observation that, among the Comanche, "Medicine" is merely a euphemism for "courage" is pertinent, for the ghost's major weapon against the neophyte doctor is fear. It is interesting that although the behavior engaged in during these four days and nights of solitude is similar to the general pattern of Plains vision questing, Sanapia conceives of this time as merely a final test and not a time when a supernatural patron could have possibly appeared to her and granted her certain supernatural prerogatives. The apparition of her patron, the eagle, would come later in her career as a doctor. In the beginning of her doctoring career, the powers which she possessed came strictly from a personal power transmission from her mother and uncle to her. Sanapia feels that visitations from either the eagle, or at times from the spirits of her mother and uncle, are gifts granted her as a reward for her faith and conscientious endeavors as a doctor.

Power Transmission

The first stage in the actual power transmission from the mother was concerned with instilling power into Sanapia's mouth and hands, the areas of the body where an eagle doctor's powers are most strongly represented. The rituals involved with this first phase of transmission are very similar to the blessing ceremony, at least in the introductory stages. Sanapia's brother was told by the mother to lay a fire of pecan wood. After the wood burned to coals, the brother brought the coals to a secluded place where Sanapia and her mother waited. The mother sat facing east, and Sanapia was instructed to sit facing her, while the mound of coals burned between them. Sanapia was cedared[1] and fanned by her mother with the standard blessings of long life and good health. This blessing also included the mother's singing of her Medicine song, an action which serves to call the *puhakut*'s power sources to his service. The mother, using her bare hand, then plucked a live coal from the mound of embers and handed it to Sanapia. At first, Sanapia reports, she balked at placing the burning coal in her hand, but at her mother's insistence she took it and was amazed that it did not burn her. She was then instructed to rub the coal over her hands. Once again the similarity in the concepts of "Medicine" and "courage" appear. Today, Sanapia interprets the handling of live coals as an act of faith in the doctor, a necessary first step in testing the potential doctor's resolve.

> I was sure scared then . . . almost got up and ran away. I was only a young girl at that time, you know. But, when I took them coals on my hand, inside and outside my hand I felt a chill, maybe. Oh, it was like chills in my hands. That has the meaning that power was in there . . . working in my hands. Felt like it would go up my arm even.

---

[1] The dried leaves of the red cedar are sprinkled on live coals, and the rising smoke is wafted over the person who is being blessed.

After Sanapia had taken the coal and covered her hands with the ashes, her mother began the transmission of supernatural power to Sanapia's mouth. Two eagle feathers, manipulated by the mother, were drawn across Sanapia's opened mouth four times; however, in the course of the fourth movement of the feathers, one of the feathers disappeared. At this occurrence Sanapia's mother told her that the eagle feather had entered her mouth and would dwell there for the rest of her life.

As with a similar phenomenon occurring in a variety of witchcraft which will be discussed in Chapter 5, Sanapia states that she does not believe that an eagle feather actually was inserted into her mouth but rather that the idea, the essence, or the Medicine which the eagle feather symbolized, was the entity which was placed in her mouth. She does not attempt to explain the disappearance of the second feather from her mother's hand except to suggest that her mother possessed certain powers which she did not transmit to Sanapia. This first phase was ended with the mother's application of red paint to Sanapia's face, forearms, and legs, from the knees to, and including, the soles of the feet.

Two tabus, or "rules" as Sanapia calls them, were attached by the mother to the powers transmitted in this first phase of the actual transmission. Sanapia was forbidden to eat any kind of fowl. Her mother warned that if she broke that rule, the feather in her throat would kill her. The second tabu forbade Sanapia to allow people to pass behind her carrying food, especially meat, while she is eating.

> That eagle, when he eats, he don't like anybody to be behind him. When its sitting on the ground, and it see anybody behind him, it twist all around and sit toward you. If he back there eating meat, he don't want any meat behind him. If some kid carry meat on a plate, it just give me chills all at once . . . you know, if they be behind me. I don't care if I don't see it, if there's meat on that plate behind me I get chills, and I know someone back there. My mother said, "If you keep it like that and try to take care of yourself, it won't make you loose your ways about it. That's going to be the rule I give you. You got to do that. Don't let anybody go behind you when you eat, especially if they carrying meat."

It is impossible to say if certain kinds of power or specific supernatural abilities to achieve a certain exclusive end were transmitted at each of the four stages of transmission. From Sanapia's discussion it can be said that each stage marked an increase in the degree of power generally. Before the beginning of the actual power transmission Sanapia was taught the ritual procedure which she would require as a doctor. The four stages of transmission acted to instill in her ever-increasing powers to successfully actualize the goals of these doctoring procedures.

An analogy can be made with the construction of an automobile. Before it is actually energized, it is equipped with everything that it will require to efficiently operate. Then, at the source of manufacture, it is carefully observed while given several rigidly controlled and graded performance tests. Supernatural power, like an untested automobile, is potentially dangerous to the operator. This appears to

be the rationale for the transmission of power in stages, each stage being inter-
rupted by a certain length of time in which the effects of the preceding stage on
the recipient can be observed. Sanapia was not entirely sure how a negative reaction to a transmission of supernatural power would manifest itself. She suggested
death or insanity as two possibilities.

For the several months following the first stage of transmission, Sanapia
was closely observed by her mother and her maternal uncle, who at this time
entered into Sanapia's training program, instructing her in the many medicinal
uses of peyote. If any ill effects from the first transmission had occurred in Sanapia,
her mother would have immediately terminated Sanapia's program and acted to
remove the power which she had given her up to that point. Sanapia's total
immersion in running water would have been a core theme of such a desacralizing
ritual. Since no negative reactions appeared in Sanapia, her mother initiated the
second stage of transmission.

All the power transmission ceremonies are generally similar in that they
are based on the blessing ceremony of the eagle doctor, which employs cedar,
eagle feathers, Medicine song, and red paint. The unique feature of the second
transmission was the mother's magical insertion of an "eagle egg" into Sanapia's
stomach. An increase in eagle traits indicates an increase in eagle power. To
Sanapia the logical pivot of the egg insertion in this second stage of transmission
is clear: "Female eagles have eggs inside them." As with the case of the eagle
feather in the first transmission ceremony, Sanapia feels that it was the essence
or the idea of the egg which entered her. Similarly, she cannot explain how the
egg disappeared from her mother's hand prior to the egg's insertion in her stomach.

Tabus

The tabu connected with this second power increase forbids Sanapia to
eat eggs. It can be seen that each stage of power increase is signaled by the neophyte
eagle doctor's acquisition of symbolic elements which are to a great degree inter-
twined with the nature of the accompanying tabus. As the power increases, the
potential dangers to the *puhakut* increase as his behavior is more tightly bound by
tabus, the breaking of which would lead to personal disaster. From Sanapia's accounts, *the puhakuts*, at least of her time, possessed a way to escape the tabu
burdens of their powers if they wished. As Sanapia grew older, she began to
acquire a craving for eggs. In order to satisfy this hunger, without risking the
dangers of breaking her "rule," she commissioned an eagle doctor to extract the
egg from her, and thus dismiss the tabu against the consumption of eggs. Of
course, by having this done she also lost the quantity of supernatural power which
accompanies the eagle egg. It is interesting to note that though the tabu was
removed, Sanapia is now physically unable to eat eggs.

Up to today, I just can't eat eggs. When I eat it I feel like it just set there
and it won't go in. I don't know why. I thought I would be able to eat eggs.
When I was small my mother won't let me eat eggs because I already had one
and she don't want me to eat eggs. But after she pass away and I start eating

eggs, but it always feel like I'm choking in here and I just quit eating them. And now I can't get the taste out of my mouth. I'll have it all day long. I just can't eat them.

Sanapia's maternal uncle gave her but one "rule." She was forbidden to eat the visceral organs of animals. This was a bitter pill for Sanapia because of her love for liver and an Indian delicacy made from stuffed intestines. She has managed to circumvent this tabu by reinterpreting it. Sanapia feels that if she changes these forbidden meats into something else, disguises them, she can eat them with no fear or guilt.

A *puhakut* cannot doctor himself in the manner which was described regarding the removal of the eagle egg. This is unfortunate for Sanapia, for as she grows older, the tabus which she must observe become increasingly cumbersome; and since she is the only living eagle doctor, she has no way in which to relieve herself of these restrictions. This is also a reason for her disinclination to associate with the less traditionally based members of the Comanche tribe. The more conservative and traditional Comanches recognizing the special limitations which are placed on Sanapia's behavior and, honoring them, make her life a little less complicated. With the less traditionally oriented, Sanapia cannot be sure that they understand the meaning of her tabus, and thus she must be constantly on guard around them lest they pass behind her while she is eating, for example, and unknowingly, or perhaps knowingly, cause her to break one of the many restrictions placed on her with regards to food and behavior. Sanapia states that ignorance is no excuse when a "rule" is broken. Her tabus are mechanical.

The unique feature in the third power transmission was Sanapia's acquisition of her Medicine song. The Medicine song is Sanapia's most direct means of communication to the supernatural realms which are the ultimate sources of her power. The song belonged to both the mother and the uncle. Sanapia considers her Medicine song extremely potent and utilizes it only under the most critical and pressing of doctoring situations. It is not a common element in her doctoring activities but is only employed when she feels that all her other tactics are failing. The song is her ultimate doctoring tool in that it is as close as she comes to actually commanding her power sources to heed her wishes.

The immediate result of her Medicine song is the summoning of the spirits of her mother and uncle. She then asks them for support in her attempts to reach more deeply into the supernaturalistic realms for more power and control over the situation which is challenging her.

When my mother gave me that song she told me, "When you come by yourself like that, when you don't have no place to go for help, when you got no one to lean on for help, sing this song. What you want, you going to get. I'll be listening to you. When you sing this song, I'm going to hear you singing and I'm going to help you."

Two tabus concerned with behavior were associated with the power increase of this third stage. Sanapia was forbidden to ever directly make a request of another. Her powers would, according to her mother, allow her to obtain anything she desired simply by wishing for it. Sanapia evades the strictures of this tabu by circumlocutions when her daily routine dictates that she must ask an individual for some object or assistance.

The second "rule" which she acquired at this stage required that she must always be alone when she doctors. Once again, Sanapia views this as a recognition of the potential dangers which excessive supernatural powers possess for humans. The only individuals who could possibly be with her while she doctors are other eagle doctors or persons who Sanapia feels have Medicine which would protect them against the dangers of supernatural contamination.

Kardiner (1945:64) makes a comment relevant at this point when writing on the subject of Comanche notions of power and magic.

Another interesting point in connection with power, probably unique with the Comanches, is that power might be obtained from the ghosts of medicine men. This was obtained through sleeping by the grave of the medicine man, not moving all night, no matter what terrifying thing happened. The ghost would then transfer the power asked for. Sometimes the sleeper would have a vision; in this the ghost did not come in human form but as a great wind and then a giant bird, which conveyed to him the power that he wanted.

Sanapia's discussion of the later stages of her training agrees with Kardiner's statement in general; however, some major divergences appear. Sanapia, through her Medicine song, is able to summon the spirits of her mother and uncle to her aid. She does not consider their appearance as the apparition of ghosts, however. To Sanapia, ghosts are totally evil entities. Ghosts are also unable to appear in human form since, in her opinion, their human forms decomposed at the place of their interment. Her mother and uncle appear to her looking exactly as they did during the time of her training. When they appear, they do not speak but rather employ hand signs to tell Sanapia that they have come to her aid.

She does not mention a Medicine man's grave as the location of the inevitable struggle with the ghosts, and she definitely does not feel that power is transmitted to her from ghosts. She does agree generally with Kardiner's mention of a "giant bird" as one of her power sources, though she does not believe that the Medicine bird is actually a ghost in another form.

In reiteration, Sanapia states that she received her initial powers through her mother and maternal uncle, and only later in her life was she honored with visitations by the eagle, her patron and guardian spirit. The four days and nights of seclusion and meditation, in her opinion, are in actuality a final test of a new doctor's ability to withstand the attacks of ghosts, and not a time when he is in a position to acquire further powers from a supernatural patron.

Final Test

Sanapia failed her final test. After her mother had explained to her what she could expect during her four-day ordeal, Sanapia was too frightened to go through with the vigil. She would spend the daylight hours sitting on the hill to which her mother had sent her, and at dusk she would creep back to her house and pass the night under the front porch. In the morning she would go back to the hill before the household had awakened. Her mother and uncle never knew about this deception. However, Sanapia believes that the great amount of sickness and misfortune experienced as a young woman can be attributed to her cowardly conduct during this last phase of her training.

Before, you have to go and fast four days, before they give you that Medicine. Maybe take a little water. You suppose to go up there on that hill and sleep up there by yourself. You suppose to pray and cry and talk. My mother say, "Somebody will come to you way in the night . . . in the middle of the night. They going to push you and kick you and they do things like that, but don't get scared. They going to kick you around and slap you. They fighting you for your Medicine." That's what they told me. But me, I was afraid to sleep up there in them mountains by myself. I didn't want to go out. I go up there and come back. Nobody come to me . . . or nothing.

Before appearing at her home on the morning of the fifth day, Sanapia bathed in a running stream as a device to erase any vestiges of supernatural residue which could be harmful to those who would greet her on her return. The mother met Sanapia as she approached the house and blessed her with the standard cedaring, fanning, and application of red paint. It was also during this blessing that the mother first addressed her daughter as *puhakut*.

Close friends of Sanapia's family had gathered at the house to congratulate Sanapia and to present her with gifts. The host family in turn gave gifts to those who came to honor Sanapia. Moccasins, blankets, shawls, groceries, money, dishes, yard goods, and horses were the items which were exchanged as gifts.

Within a few days after Sanapia returned from her four-day fasting, her family sponsored a peyote meeting. The main function of this particular meeting was to gather a large group of Comanches for the purpose of formally announcing Sanapia's newly acquired status. Also, it was thought that the prayers which would be offered for her during the meeting would aid her to more easily bear the burdens which her power imposed. The morning after the meeting was festive, consisting of more gift giving and feasting. However, at the same time that the beginning of Sanapia's new career was being celebrated, her mother's doctoring career had ended. The mother, though retaining all her powers, would cease to function as a doctor. Her withdrawal, however, was voluntary. If she had so desired, she could have continued her doctoring activities. This type of behavior would have been considered improper on the part of the mother, even though Sanapia would not be able to doctor until many years in the future, after menopause. Sanapia, basing her actions on those of her mother, will also cease doctoring once she has transmitted her skills and powers to her successor. In the nomadic Comanche culture, power could be transmitted from donor to recipient with no loss on the part of the donor. This is the case with the transmission of power from the mother to Sanapia.

In Sanapia's accounts of her mother's temper during the time of transmission of power, it would seem that the mother, who had reached a very advanced age, was tired of her profession and its rigors. She felt, perhaps, that she could excuse her inactivity in doctoring to the fact that her daughter possessed her powers. In other words, the mother's behavior could possibly have been based on circumstance, though Sanapia now interprets it as a law to be observed in transmission of power from a donor to a recipient. Sanapia is also in agreement that this type of rule does not make good sense. However, she explains that she does not understand many things which she does in her capacity as doctor. It is enough for Sanapia that her mother and uncle told her to keep the Medicine way, so she attempts to keep it, even if she does not understand certain aspects of the role she inherited. A practical aspect of what Sanapia considers one of the more senseless of her rules of behavior concerns the method she must follow in choosing a successor. As a woman, her first choice of successor would be her favorite daughter. However, at this point if she gave her Medicine to her daughter and then ceased doctoring herself, as she feels she must, it would be approximately twenty years before the Comanches would again have an eagle doctor in their midst, that is, until after the daughter passes menopause. During this time the special prerogatives of her Medicine way could probably be taken over by peyotism, as she has seen occur among the neighboring Kiowa. It is significant that she does consider herself in competition with peyote doctors.

Those Kiowa got this old man that doctors with peyote but he don't get people with twisted-face well . . . sometimes he don't get anybody well. That's what I heard. I even got some of those peoples that go to him . . . they come to me later on and I fix them up. Peyote is good but some things can't get well with it. I can do things that they can't do because I got that power. People learn that and then I see them . . . come to me. Us Comanches got two brothers that doctor with peyote too. That's all they use. There's a young man down at Walters but nobody pay him any attention. He just says he got power but I want to know where he got it from. Nobody knows that so . . . well, he's just a young man.

Dreams and Visions

Shortly after Sanapia began her doctoring career, she had her first "real dream." She distinguishes between ordinary dreams, which she considers generally unimportant, and real dreams, to which she attributes enough importance that she will be motivated to certain kinds of behavior by them. The first dream experience occurred after she appealed to the eagle, while doctoring, to supply her with a special Medicine feather.

This man, something like a man, came to where I was sleeping way in the night. He stood there and then held his hand to me. I just watch him, you know. I wasn't scared or nothing. Then he move his arm toward north and all at once I saw his arm go away from him. And next morning I said, "You all know what, I'm sure lonesome to see my uncle. He's up north around Geary. Let's go see him, if you all want to." Here we pack up and beat it down there north. And we was coming. We visit him about four days or five days. I said, "Uncle, we going home now." He said, "Why?" and I told him, "Just feel I get home and get my check." Then he went back and opened up his suitcase and said, "Come here," and I went. He had about twelve eagle feathers and he told me to take one I want best. I pulled out the best one in the bunch, and he said, "That's for you. Take it with you." And so that feather, what I dream about was given to me by my uncle. That's what that dream, really good dream, carried with it.

A recurring real dream comes to Sanapia which, in its essentials, is similar to the one just mentioned. The man appears to her at night and extends his hand to her. In the palm of his hand is, a peyote button which covers the entire area of his palm, even fusing with his hand. He instructs Sanapia to take it from him. Her first several efforts are futile, for as she reaches for the peyote, it disappears. Finally, she is successful in taking the peyote from the man's hand. As soon as she grasps it in both hands, the peyote enters her hands and spreads a chill or tingling sensation through her hands and arms. Sanapia equates the tingling sensation with supernatural power.

Sanapia is not consistent in statements concerning her opinion of the identity of the man in her real dreams. At times she identifies him as the spirit of her maternal uncle, at times as "something that's helping," and at other times as the "peyote man." The identity of the man seems of little concern to her. The significant part of the dream to her is her magical acquisition of the peyote's power.

During peyote meetings she has had several experiences which she considers similar to her real dreams. The central theme of all these peyote experiences is the same: The peyote tells Sanapia that through its power she can accomplish anything she desires. The following account is typical. It also contains, once again, the peyote–hand motif. The gigantic size she attains relative to those around her is another recurring element in these peyote experiences.

And you know, that night, oh, I ate so much of that peyote, and I just feel good. Then, when I look, all the people sitting around in the tepee like that, everybody was way down right under my feet, and I was above them. I was sitting on top of them. That's how the peyote affect me in my body. And I said, "I wonder why they sitting down there and me sitting up here?" And I look this way and my boy was sitting here and I said, "Look at these peoples sitting down there and I'm sitting up here. Here's your head right here and you're sitting way down there too. I wonder why?" He said, "Mama, you eat too much of that peyote." And you know, I close my eyes and when I look at my hand, I had a big peyote there, as big as my hand. It was just sitting there, I said, "Look son, look what I got. Look at this peyote." He said, "Mama, I don't see anything there." But everytime I look, there it is. It was great peyote with green and with real pretty designs on it. And somehow it said, "Go ahead, use this and you could just do anything you want with it. You could just doctor anybody you want and they going to be alright. Right now you could doctor that one." But he didn't name anybody out. Come into my mind like that. "Right now you could just go out there and do as you please with this peyote. You infected with it so strong you could just raise a sick-bed man or woman or child. You could raise a dead man." It just came into my mind like that.

Visitations from the Medicine Eagle

Sanapia has had only two visitations from her supernatural eagle patron in her doctoring career. Both occurred during doctoring situations as a direct result of the singing of her Medicine song. Sanapia reports that her Medicine eagle looks like eagles she has seen in the wild except that it is much larger. She can feel her eagle's presence before she sees it. On the first occasion she felt a rush of air from its wings, and on the second it was a tingling sensation which announced the presence of the Medicine eagle. Sanapia states that when the eagle came to her, everything around her dissappeared with the resultant image: an eagle against a murky gray background. These visitations were very brief. During the eagle's apparition, it appeared to be hovering directly in front of her at a distance of about 4 or 5 feet. While the eagle was present, Sanapia trembled violently and perspired freely. She states that her heart beat very rapidly and she felt as if she was going to faint.

Contacts with the Supernatural

Sanapia has provided herself with several contacts with the supernatural worlds. Since she cannot visit the other worlds, Sanapia must depend on these contacts to assist her in making her wishes known to the supernatural realms. Her comments concerning her Medicine song clearly identify the spirits of her mother and maternal uncle as her two major assistants. It should also be remembered that she considers her Medicine song as her most potent piece of doctoring paraphernalia. The spirit–man in her recurring real dreams is also a liaison or avenue of rapport between Sanapia and the supernatural, though in this case it is strictly a one-way phenomenon which is beyond Sanapia's control.

Sanapia's eagle comes to her only through the intercession of her mother and uncle via Sanapia's Medicine song. She associates her lack of courage in the final phase of her doctor training with her inability to call the eagle to her aid independently of her mother's and uncle's intercession. This is also the reason why Sanapia possesses only one Medicine song instead of the many which her mother and uncle possessed. In the final analysis, Sanapia can rarely act independently as a doctor; she must call on the assistance of her teachers. Therefore, instead of having many songs for summoning power, she has one. She must first call on her mother and uncle and then relate to them her wishes, which they, through their superior powers, actualize. Basically, then, Sanapia's real power is the control which she can exert over the powerful spirits of two *puhakuts*. However, this type of analysis is foreign to Sanapia. She prefers to think of herself as the pitiable supplicant.

Peyote is another important liaison with supernatural powers. The power she receives from peyote is the only power which she can manipulate entirely independently of the spirits of her mother and uncle. Still, the power of peyote is subordinate to the powers possessed by the spirits of her mother and uncle, and in her most difficult doctoring situations and in all her most criticial moments, it is to the spirits of her teachers that she turns for aid.

The Supernatural Universe

Sanapia's description of the supernatural universe is full of contradictory elements. This is not as great an obstacle to action as it may seem since she addresses each element individually as the situation demands. She has no need to attempt to grasp the entirety of this universe at once. Sanapia is able to select from her potpourri of supernaturalistic notions the ones which best suit a particular occasion.

She believes that living human beings share the earth with the ghosts, or malevolent spirits of deceased humans who, alive, led evil lives. The ghosts can enter into the world of men, but men cannot enter the world of ghosts except through death. Also, somewhere, neither in the plane of living man nor in the plane of ghost existence, is the realm of pure, unembodied supernatural power. Such entities as the sun, the earth, and the eagle are able to tap this power and thus possess it to a greater extent than can mortal men. Power can be acquired by men only through secondhand channels and never from its source. A mortal would be killed if exposed to pure power. The power, from its original source, is inexhaustible.

In yet another plane of existence are found the spirits of good men such as the disciples of Jesus and the spirits of Sanapia's mother and uncle. This realm is not quite like heaven, which is the abode of God and Jesus and the eternal home of those ordinary souls who have nothing to offer the world of the living, as do the spirits of Medicine men or the disciples of Jesus. Hell is somewhere deep in the earth. Sanapia believes that it is the special eternal home of evil white men. Her notions of the nature of hell follow the standard Christian concept.

Peyote is similar to the sun or the eagle in its ability to embody an extraordinary degree of supernatural power. However, unlike the sun or the eagle, peyote comes from the Christian God as a sign of his love for all Indian people. According to Sanapia, the sun has existed longer then the Christian God, and is therefore entirely self-sufficient.

Thus Sanapia can become more or less Christian, peyotist, or Plains shaman as varying situations present themselves. By not assigning a negative value to contradictory elements in her supernaturalistic universe and by oversimplifying the similarities, Sanapia possesses a flexibility which confounds any attempt to present a very cogent description of her "religion." If a key pervasive theme had to be chosen, it probably would be concerned with the idea of supernatural power and the desirability of its acquisition and control.

A Successor

At the present time Sanapia is beginning to consider the problem of a successor, for she feels that her doctoring career is rapidly approaching its final hours. There does not seem to be a very rigid or fixed system for the selection of a successor. A Medicine woman should transmit her powers to a favorite daughter, and a Medicine man, to an eldest son. However, if the first choice does not respond or does not demonstrate the required personal qualities, he is eliminated.

Sanapia's daughter has shown little interest in acquiring her mother's powers. Sanapia feels that this is because her daughter is "too much like a white man." Sanapia's youngest son has already tried and failed in his attempt to acquire his mother's power because Sanapia did not believe in his sincerity. Thus, he is permanently eliminated. Sanapia's next choice was her daughter's adolescent son, though Sanapia fears that the mother's influence will eventually rule him out as a potential successor.

During the final stages of my research with Sanapia, a new potential successor presented himself—Sanapia's eldest son. She had not even considered him in her search for a successor because of his aversion for all those things which are associated with traditionalist Comanche society. Recently, however, in his late forties, he has begun to take a greater interest in peyotism, for example, and in acquiring from his mother a more thorough command of the Comanche language. He also embodies all those personal traits which Sanapia feels a doctor should possess.

> You know that oldest boy of mine down at Lawton? He sure is a good one. He never say anthing out of the way about anybody. He's just so happy right now. And everytime I go down there, I see somebody at his house. He takes them in to help them along some. He gives them his last dollar. He sure likes to help people out. And he treats me real good too. Everybody seem to like him. I talk to him about my doctoring ways and he said that he would think about it and tell me later on sometime.

Sanapia can transmit her knowledge of medicines or actually dispense medicines to anyone for a fee; however, the transmission of power, since it is received as a gift, must be given as a gift. Once again, this follows from Sanapia's feeling that power cannot actually be owned by an individual. A person may acquire the knowledge required to manipulate power to a certain degree; however, this is the only sense in which he actually owns it. When a *puhakut* dies, the power he "possesses" does not die with him but once again becomes a free, unattached, and available agent to the next man or woman who has the ability to control or manipulate it. To Sanapia, man is subordinate to supernatural power. It would be illogical to her to conceive of a weaker agent controlling a stronger agent. Power can temporarily enter a mortal and become one with him, but it is still in the position of ultimate control. She cites the many tabus which a *puhakut* must observe, and mentions that there are no restrictions placed on the power.

She will state that power increases through time. A further probing of this notion reveals that what she means is that a *puhakut*, through time and experience, can become more efficient in manipulating power. Sanapia conceives of supernatural power as a static phenomenon. Once it is established, it does not decrease or increase of its own accord.

The tabus which are attached to supernatural power are a major reason that a doctor may experience difficulty in his attempt to find a successor. Wallace and Hoebel (1952:165) mention this in their discussion of Comanche supernaturalism:

> Such reluctance to assume power, or particular powers, was common among the Comanches. Powers were always accompanied by tabus; tabus were onerous restrictions on the freedom of action that a Comanche male cherished. The result was an ambivalent attitude toward the possession of Medicine.

Sanapia, being aware of this, is planning to delete certain tabus from her Medicine way in order to make the acquisition of her powers more palatable to a twentieth-century Comanche. Of course, the absence of certain tabus also indicates the absence of the concomitant degree of power. Her successor will not be burdened with the food and eating tabus which Sanapia finds so cumbersome. He will also not have to be bothered with the tabu forbidding the making of direct requests. These deletions are major concessions for Sanapia, but ones which she feels are necessary if her tradition is to continue.

Sanapia's mother modified her Medicine way before transmitting it to Sanapia for much the same reasons that Sanapia is now being compelled to consider. An element which occurred in her mother's modifications, though not in Sanapia's, was the deletion of certain powers because of their lack of contemporary function. Her mother possessed many medicines and songs which were associated with the role of midwife. She told Sanapia that the delivering of infants would be taken over by white doctors in the future and, therefore, there was no reason for Sanapia to learn the skill or to be compelled to observe the tabus associated with it. To both Sanapia and her mother the primary function of an eagle doctor is his ability to cure ghost sickness[2]. The deletions in tabus and power made by Sanapia and her mother have not infringed on this specific power.

Sanapia believes that her doctoring tradition will ultimately die as the Comanches become more acculturated. She states that *puhakuts* will cease to exist when the Comanches have no more need for them. Sanapia's sensitivity, concern with function, and general pragmatic instincts make her a very sensitive barometer of the manner in which culture change is viewed and handled by a traditionally oriented Comanche. Since her opinion of herself is bound by supernatural sanctions, and not merely by elusive value structure, her reaction to culture change is much more dramatic.

Attitudes about Sanapia

The ways in which Comanches of both northern and southern affiliation and members of neighboring tribes react to Sanapia as a personality are many and

---

[2] "Ghost sickness," "twisted face," and "crooked mouth" are names which the Comanches, as well as other southern Plains tribes, give to a condition of facial hemiplegia, usually with concomitantly occurring constrictions of the hands and arms, which is said to result from ghost contact.

varied. Because of her supernatural powers and mercurial temperament, a certain aloofness marks her relationship even with her friends. Only two old women, women who grew up with Sanapia, seem to be able to overcome this barrier. This aloofness is as much instigated by Sanapia as it is a reaction of others based on fear, or at least uneasiness in her presence.

Some Comanches exhibit a type of reaction to Sanapia which is interpreted by other Comanches as jealousy. Sanapia has a position and a skill which is denied to the majority of Comanches. Many of the younger and more acculturated though sympathetic Comanches consider her a likeable but eccentric old woman. She is considered ridiculous by many of the southern Comanches. Many Comanches, as well as neighboring Kiowas and Apaches, continue to represent her as sexually promiscuous, alcoholic, violent, and prone to excessive gambling. However, in all these cases her traditionalism and conservative Comanche beliefs are acknowledged, though they may be interpreted positively or negatively, depending on who is presenting the opinion.

A Kiowa woman offered the following opinion:

She sure is a good old woman . . . pretty for an old woman too. I seen you with her bunch a lot so I guess you know what she is . . . what she does. I took my niece up to her once and she cared for her and got her well in a few days. I tell other people about how she took care of my little girl and they might go to see her if they get sick bad or if their family might get sick.

Another informant was less charitable in his evaluation:

I don't know much about it. I've heard some of my people talking about an old woman who lives south from here. They say she can curse you if she wants to and make you sick. It's that woman you mention too. She supposed to be a bad one, but I never seen her. I don't believe that suff about curses myself but a lot of people . . . Indian people . . . do. You better watch out. They say she can do it.

Sanapia's Self-Concept

Sanapia is aware that some people laugh at her, and she does as much as she can to eliminate this possibility, for she is an exceedingly proud woman. Types of behavior which ostentatiously identify her as a *puhakut*, such as wearing a black kerchief or vocally demanding that others observe her tabu restrictions, are avoided by her for fear that others will think that she is "just a crazy old Indian."

Sanapia's opinion of herself remains quite high in spite of the pressures that surround her. In the following account she describes how she brought a dead niece back to life:

I was doctoring my niece one time . . . the doctor gave up on her. She had cancer and liver. So the doctor, white doctor, gave up. They dismissed her from the Indian hospital and she went home. Somebody came to our house that after-

noon and told us that L——— was dying. The doctor gave up. I told my husband, "Let's go see her." And we beat it down there and it was about five o'clock,
late that afternoon. It was cold. When we got there she was just lying on her
back like that . . . nobody was in the house except her. Her husband was gone
and her children were all gone. She was white as a sheet. Her face was just
white and her lips were blue. She didn't even notice me come in. I wake her
up and said, "Are you sleeping? What's the matter with you?" She said, "I'm
dying . . . going to die tonight. That's what the doctor told me. They dismissed
me from the hospital. I'm going to die either tonight or tomorrow . . . just
any day. Could you help me?" That's what she said. And I told J———, "You
go get your brothers. I'll get her out of it . . . that's nothing. That cancer ain't
nothing to me." And he beat it down there to his brothers and they come in
right after dark. That night we soaked that deer hide . . . soaked it in water
till it could get soft and they put it on the drum. And right there in the middle
of town . . . she got a home in the middle of town and a lot of white people
living all around her house. So I said, "Let's have this peyote meeting for her
tonight . . . drum all night. Let me fix her up. She be alright." And so that
night we had a drumming right there in the middle of town. And she was worse
the next morning. I said, "This is too noisy. I don't like to doctor anybody in
noisy place. Let's take her home." So we load her up and brought her down
here to our place. That night we had another peyote meeting inside of the
house and it was just pouring down rain and we had the meeting for her. Took
that peyote and said, "Our fathers, way back in years . . . our grandfathers took
this medicine, and they said that whenever anybody sick like that you just take
this and chew it and then put it in your hands and let her swallow it . . . give
her four at the start." And I done that. I prayed and I talked to that peyote
just like I'm talking to you. I said, "If you don't get her well, I don't want you.
If you not nothing, if you ain't got power, I don't want to use you anymore."
God made me in this world and he gave me this power just like when he was
here on land. Jesus went around blessing people and healing the sick and
everything like that and I believe that I got the power in my hands. I believe
I could get her well. So that night we had a peyote meeting and the second
night we had another one and the fourth night . . . the fourth night she died.
She just went out. She was blue . . . fingernails were blue and her lips turn
blue. I told them, "Take that drum hide out." And they took it, rinse it out,
squeeze it, and I said, "Give it to me." And I put it on her head. I rub her
face with it, and four times I done that to her and then I sing my Medicine
song. When anybodys dying and I doctor them that's the only time I sing that
special song I got. So I said, "You all carry her and put her on my bed," and
they carried her. I said, "You all stay out there in the front room." And they
all stayed out there and it was still pouring rain. Everybody get out. It was
raining out there and the wind was howling around. I sing this song and I fan
her and I doctor her . . . give her that medicine. I don't know how many
times I give her that. And after awhile she open her eyes and said, "I'm sure
thirsty." And after that she got alright.

Sanapia considers herself a slightly outmoded necessity in Comanche society.
She knows that she represents an extremely ancient Comanche institution, and
it is in that knowledge that her feeling of uniqueness rests; at the same time she
can foresee the final end of her tradition. Many times, as we sat watching auto-
mobiles moving along a highway or observed the skyscrapers in Oklahoma City
and Wichita, she would speak of the incongruity of herself and the twentieth-
century world in which she lives.

I just can't think how it came this way. Look at them cars. I remember when I never seen them before. And all those white peoples walking along, and those big buildings all around here. I don't like it here. My grandmother said this way would come and now here I am and she died long time back in years. Maybe I should be with her now because my way is getting no good up to today. Maybe I should be dead too. Even my own kids growing up like white peoples, and they think I'm just a funny old woman. I know they do! But I ain't got too many more years to go yet. And here, you, a white person, asking me all those old ways and my kids go around here and there and don't even talk to me about those things. It sure is funny, ain't it?

3

Medicine Kit

Care of Medicines

SANAPIA KEEPS the various kinds of botanical and nonbotanical medicines which she utilizes in a leather "travel case." This case is kept on a shelf on the west wall of her bedroom. She will also only open her medicine kit on the west end of a room or tent. The medicines in the travel case are kept orderly and fully stocked at all times to facilitate speed in an emergency call on her services. Each medicine is wrapped in a piece of cloth. The cloth is black in almost every instance, though Sanapia states that this is only coincidence. In the inside lid of the case she keeps her Medicine feather—a tail feather of a golden eagle.

Sanapia is the only one allowed to touch this box or its contents, and she will not open it in the presence of small children or menstruating women. The medicine kit is potentially very dangerous if handled in an incorrect manner or by the wrong person. Sanapia recalls what happened to the niece of an eagle doctor who died several years ago.

> When S——— died, a niece got into her medicine bag. Now don't you know she sure shouldn't done that. But it got her . . . she got that twisted face and nobody fix her . . . couldn't do a thing for her. If she had sense, she would take that bag, don't open it mind you, and throw it in the creek. Then it couldn't hurt nobody.

Running water, because of its desacralizing effect, is Sanapia's only remedy by which the possible harm produced by an individual's inadvertent contamination by supernatural power or Medicine belonging to another can be undone. In a doctoring situation if it is absolutely necessary that another person touch some object connected with her medicine kit, this person must immediately be cedared, or "smoked," upon completion of the task; that is, the dried and rubbed leaves of the red cedar are sprinkled on live coals and the rising smoke is drawn over the contaminated person in a ritual cleansing act. After the cedar ritual

47

someone must pour a ladle of water over each of his hands four times. The one who pours the water over the hands of the one contaminated and who aids in the cedaring may be any person present except, of course, a small child or a menstruating woman.

Sanapia forbids children near her medicines because she feels that such close proximity could make a child sick, cause him bad luck, or possibly kill him. She is not quite sure why the medicine could hurt a child, but she is sure about another aspect of the danger which her medicines present to children. Her special and unique power is ghost Medicine. She feels that ghosts therefore hate her and are constantly attempting to harm her and those close to her. This means that they are very likely near her most of the time, especially when she is working her Medicine against them or the results of their activity. Though they cannot harm her or adults who have courage to resist them, they can harm children, who are naturally weaker than adults in courage and Medicine.

With respect to her aversion to the presence of menstruating women while she is doctoring or when her medicines are open, she can offer no specific rationale except that these were the instructions she received from her mother. The only possible explanation which she felt she could offer is that loss of blood means weakness, and weakness makes an individual more susceptible to illness caused by supernatural or natural means.

Wallace and Hoebel (1952:158) write that among the Comanche all medicine had to be protected against contamination by grease as well as the presence of menstruating women. It is interesting that Sanapia is not concerned about the possible ill effects of grease near her medicines. In fact, when directly questioned about her reaction if her medicines actually came in contact with grease, she replied that she would simply wipe it off.

Nonbotanical Medicines

Approximately half of the contents of Sanapia's medicine kit is composed of medicines of a nonbotanical nature.

Crow Feathers

Four tail feathers from a crow are tied at their base to form a loose bundle and are hung near the door of a house as a protective amulet against ghosts. Sanapia states that the power in the crow feathers is intrinsic to the feathers and does not depend on her handling of them to give them this capacity. She always utilizes this amulet when she doctors because of her belief that ghosts are especially numerous when she begins to make Medicine against them. This amulet, therefore, aids her to dispel ghosts and acts to protect the house and its occupants from the evil designs of the angered ghosts.

Sanapia could offer no explanation as to why the ghost should fear these feathers. A Kiowa informant, who uses crow feathers in much the same manner as Sanapia, explained that ghosts sometimes appear at night as owls. The crow and the owl are natural enemies. By using crow feathers in this manner, one is enlisting the crow's aid against the owls or ghosts. Sanapia, however, does not share her Kiowa and Apache neighbor's aversion to owls.

You know, these Apaches sure are crazy. They get scared of them owls . . . they might hear them holler or something. It ain't nothing but a funny bird. A bird can't hurt nobody and they think it's a ghost.

Glass Slivers

Slivers of glass, usually obtained from broken beer bottles, are used by Sanapia whenever a certain treatment calls for the making of incisions in the flesh. This operation is almost always immediately succeeded by the use of the sucking horn or by suction applied by mouth.

Several examples will adequately explain the function of these slivers of brown glass. For both a severe headache and extreme vertigo the same procedure is followed. Minute cuts are made at either temple, in the middle of the forehead, and immediately below the hairline at the nape of the neck. These incisions are approximately one-sixteenth of an inch in length and penetrate only deep enough to produce a blood flow. The sucking horn is applied after all the cuts have been made, and sucking is continued from point to point around the head until both Sanapia and the patient are satisfied with the results.

Sanapia believes that "bad blood," or "foamy stuff," causing pressure in the head area is the cause of both conditions. To relieve the symptoms, the blood, or foamy stuff, must be removed. The same notion of pain caused by the pressure of expanding foamy stuff stimulates the use of the cutting operation in the treatment of swollen joints, which Sanapia calls "rheumatism" in the absence of evidence indicating breaks or sprains.

Sanapia specifies the use of only brown glass in an attempt to imitate her mother. The mother utilized what, from Sanapia's description, appear to have been brown flintlike slivers as cutting tools in doctoring. Sanapia does not know how to obtain "cutting rocks" so she employs brown glass as a close approximation.

Sucking Horn

Sanapia's sucking horn is a 4-inch section of the horn casing of a variety of domestic cattle found in her vicinity. The 4-inch section is cut from the point or extremity of the horn. This piece of horn is usually drilled and scoured to develop a clear opening from the tip of the segment of horn, which will be used as the mouthpiece, to the termination of the horn or area of widest diameter, which will be the point of application when the horn is employed in doctoring.

This item is used when the treatment calls for Sanapia to attempt to suck sickness from the body of her patient. She recalls that when she was young, the sucking horn was used very little by the Comanche doctors which she had the opportunity to observe. If the treatment called for suction, the doctor employed his mouth. Sanapia believes that it was with the advent of the white man and his teaching that many diseases are spread and caught via the mouth that Comanche doctors began to depend more on the sucking horn in an effort to keep their mouth from contact with the patient.

Charcoal from a Peyote Drum

Before the drumhead is attached to the drum used in the ceremonies of the Native American Church, the drum body is filled approximately one-third full with water. Several small pieces of charcoal from any source immediately available are placed in the water, and the head is then attached. The charcoal and water play important parts in the morning rituals held at the close of Comanche peyote meetings. Both the water and the charcoal are considered blessed by their presence in the meeting and are thought to possess certain sacred qualities. Because of the power which Sanapia feels pervades the charcoal from the peyote drum, she considers this charcoal desirable as a medicine.

The charcoal from the drum is given to Sanapia after peyote meetings which have been held on her property. She uses these fragments in several ways. To contain the movement or spread of any kind of pain or to prohibit the spread of swelling caused by such conditions as snakebite or sprains, she encloses the afflicted area in a circle drawn on the patient's skin with this charcoal. Also, in doctoring a particularly difficult case, she sometimes rubs this charcoal on her palms to supplement her power.

White Otter Fur

Sanapia learned the use of a type of fur, which she states comes from a white otter, as a medicine from a Shoshone woman during one of her visits to the Wind River Shoshone communities around Fort Washakie, Wyoming. This is specificically used to treat illnesses in infants, which are felt to be localized in the infant's head. Sanapia cuts a small square from this pelt and places it on live coals. As the smoke rises from this smoldering fur, she holds the infant over the coals and moves him through the rising smoke four times. This medicine smoke is believed to enter the infant's head, where it's curative qualities work their effects. An Arapaho-Comanche uncle of Sanapia states that weasel tails are also used in this manner by the Comanches.

Porcupine Quills

Porcupine quills are used in the treatment of children in much the same manner as white fur. Four of the quills are deposited on coals. The infant is then passed through the rising smoke four times. Sanapia states:

Sometimes they say kids get lonesome . . . when they sick, they just lonesome. Those stickers are good for that. They have medicine to help little children when I use them.

Bone Medicine

Sanapia calls this medicine *piamupits*, which she translates as "big old giant." She also refers to it as *tsunhip*, a Comanche word for "bone." Wallace and Hoebel (1952:171) write concerning this medicine:

The madstone, or medicine bone was used for wounds, infections, boils, and pains. It was a small piece of leg bone of the giant prehistoric mammoth believed by the Comanches to be the bones of *piamɜmpits*—the cannibal owl. Placed over the affected spot, it was supposed to draw out the poison.

Sanapia offers the following description of what *piamupits* was supposed to have looked like.

It look like a man . . . big, old monster. They said it got a face like a man. It's got hair all over its body and it got big feet. It's tall, you know. They die of old age, I guess. They be way out there somewhere and just sit there and die. Just after awhile dirt just covering them up, and they go under ground like that. That's where they find this medicine up to today.

Sanapia grinds this medicine, which she calls "bone medicine," into a powder and mixes it with water to form a dilute medicinal solution. She sometimes simply wets the piece of bone and applies it to the afflicted area of the body. Bone medicine is used to strengthen bones and is especially effective in the treatment of sprains. Sanapia does not mention its use in the treatment of boils, wounds, or infections.

The Bible

Sanapia carries a Bible with her most of the time, and it is always present when she doctors. Before beginning treatment she holds the Bible in both hands before her and prays for power.

I really read bible lots, and I go by the bible when I'm doctoring too. I always ask God to give power to my hands and mind. I pray hard to the Holy Ghost. I learned that bible while I was at Cache Creek school. My mother didn't go by the bible when she doctoring, but I do, because you got to ask God for help sometimes.

Medicine Feather

Sanapia's Medicine feather is the tail feather from a golden eagle. She employs it in every case she doctors, and of all the items which she carries when she doctors, this is the most revered. The feather is used to ceremonially "fan" her patient at various points during the course of treatment and as a general prop in her doctoring performances. It is always cedared before and after use.

"Fanning" is an act of blessing as well as a strictly curative act when performed by Sanapia. When it is being used as a tool in the doctoring procedure, she employs the feather to waft the smoke from certain smoldering medicines over her patient. At times though, during treatment and always immediately after treatment, Sanapia lightly taps the patient with her Medicine feather around the face and head, making four passes over the face and forehead and four passes over the back of the head. She then taps four times on each arm with a fanning motion. This is proceeded by four fanlike taps on the chest and back and four fanning passes over the front and back of the body from the waist down. Sanapia prays that her patient may live a long, healthy life as she fans him and that all evil will be blown away from the patient by the motion of the feather. She explains that she has the power of the eagle; and when she touches a person with her Medicine feather, it is as if the eagle were touching them, instilling in them some of its Medicine. Her feather carries with it the tabus associated with her other medicine articles. However, a specific emphasis was placed by her mother on the prohibition of taking the Medicine feather into a room or area in which there is a large group of people.

> That eagle got some kind of power that I use for Medicine. I got one eagle feather, and it is really powerful, that thing. And I believe it. I done many works with that feather. I believe it.

Indian Lard

"Indian lard" is the name Sanapia applies to tallow or rendered beef fat. She uses it as a general purpose salve, though she states that it is especially efficacious in the treatment of severe burns. Also, it is her only remedy for constipation. Two or three tablespoonsful of lukewarm liquified tallow are administered to a patient with constipation.

Mouth Wash

The majority of cases which Sanapia treats involve the sucking operation. When the sucking is completed, Sanapia requires something to kill the "poison" and the disagreeable taste which is left in her mouth. Her mother used kerosene; however, Sanapia prefers a commercial brand of mouth wash and carries a small bottle of it in her medicine kit.

Red Paint

The red paint used by Sanapia is obtained by grinding and powdering a dark red clay which she finds west of Geary, Oklahoma. The paint is reconstituted by mixing it with water or tallow.

The paint is ever present in all of her blessing ceremonies. She also uses this paint at the termination of her treatment of ghost sickness. On the last day of treatment, she paints the patient's face, lower arms, and lower legs. The patient is instructed to wear the paint for two days before washing it off.

Sanapia states that painting is a prayer to the earth. The red paint is obtained from the earth and is the color of the earth. When she applies it to her patient she is asking the earth to care for him.

> The earth . . . talk to it like a mother. They call it that. Say "Watch this man, or woman, or child. They walking on you, same color as you, they you child. You can see that. Watch out for them during the long time they got to be on you."

Black Kerchief

Sanapia keeps most of her medicines wrapped in pieces of black material which are commercially sold as women's head scarfs. These large black squares of cloth are also used by some males as Western-style ties. When Sanapia is traveling without her medicine kit, though carrying her Medicine feather, she keeps it wrapped in a black kerchief.

The black kerchief, worn knotted at the throat, is a customary sign among the Comanches and neighboring tribes of a possessor of Medicine. Sanapia was instructed to always wear the black kerchief as a symbol of her powers. She does not wear this badge today for fear of ridicule. Sanapia does, however, keep a black kerchief tied to the headboard of her bed. She states that black is the color of luck and good fortune. She also adds that it indicates to ghosts that the wearer is not afraid of their powers.

The black kerchief, or piece of black cloth, can be used in doctoring to cover the patient's face when he is instructed to inhale medicine smoke. Sanapia sometimes uses the black kerchief in this manner during the doctoring of ghost sickness.

Sanapia collecting medicines, 1967.

Botanical Medicines: Collection, Preparation, and Dosage

Sanapia collects her botanical medicines from their natural habitat in the late fall and early winter. She feels that by this late date the rattlesnakes, of which she has a morbid fear, will be less numerous. More importantly, she feels that plants are not completely matured until immediately before their death at the first frost of fall.

I don't know how you could get any medicines in the spring. Just full grown is when they any good. That's when I get it. Rattlesnakes be gone too. In the fall they be already to get. Go get them when its cool, now its no good because it's summer. Too hot and too many snakes around. Plants aren't good now anyway for medicine.

The root is the most important source of medicine on any plant, according to Sanapia. She seldom utilizes other parts of a plant, but it is noteworthy that when she does, the part she uses is in almost every instance the top of the plant.

Sanapia feels that the two most important sources of power for a medicine plant are the earth and the sun. She uses this rationale to explain her use of only the extreme top of plants, the part nearest the sun, and the extremity most surrounded by earth, the root. Peyote and cedar are notable exceptions to this scheme.

Bottom, left to right: medicine cedar, sucking horn, bakumak. *Top, left to right: peyote, glass slivers,* bekwinatsu.

However, these plants are believed to possess a high degree of power by their nature and are therefore not so dependent on the earth and the sun for power.

In the fall when Sanapia judges that the sun is growing weaker and is less able to give power to the medicine plants, she begins her medicine plant collection. She feels she is then obtaining the medicines at their peak of maturity. In the case of my investigation of Sanapia, her collecting time fell in late October and early November. The later the summer and fall, the more efficacious the medicine plants will be since they have been exposed to the sun for an added amount of time.

For the most part the plants which Sanapia uses grow in sandy soil. She denies that medicine plants can be obtained from any other type of soil. *Basiwa:pi* is the word which Sanapia applies to this type of soil, and she translates the word as "sandy;" "sandy ground;" or "best ground."

Sanapia follows a fairly rigid field preparation of the medicine plants she collects. As soon as possible after extracting them from the earth, they are taken to the nearest body of flowing water, where they are cut into manipulatable sizes and washed. Upon returning to her house, she once again washes the medicines and then stores them in the storm cellar, suspending some from lines which traverse the cellar and placing the remainder in jars. The immersion in flowing water applies to roots or plant parts other than leaves or flowering bodies;

Bottom: sweet sage. Left to right: mescal beans, chow feather amulet, charcoal from peyote drum, gray sage.

Sanapia preparing medicine.

but since Sanapia almost exclusively uses only the root of the plant for medicine, this concern with flowing water seems ubiquitous on medicine-plant-collecting trips.

Her dosages of the various botanical medicines follow the mystical number four found in the southern Plains area. The medicinal decoctions and infusions which she prepares are always given in units of four—four cupsful, four spoonsful, and so forth. Her externally applied medicines, such as salves and liniments, are administered with four movements of the hand; and when dried cedar leaves are employed to produce medicine smoke, they are deposited on the live coals in the course of four consecutive abbreviated motions of the hand.

In the following discussions, a standardized introductory line will be used for each plant when possible. The Comanche term for the plant will be presented first, followed by Sanapia's translation of the Comanche term. The English translation of the Comanche term will be followed by the binomial classification of the plant, which in turn will be followed by the English common name.

ekapokowa:pi

"red berry cedar"   *Juniperus pinchotii*   (red cedar; juniper)

Sanapia refers to all other varieties of *Juniperus* as *taiβowa:pi*, or "white man cedar." She uses the dried and pulverized root to make a decoction which is internally administered to treat menstrual complaints. However, to Sanapia, the dried and rubbed leaves of the cedar are the most important parts of the plant. She sprinkles them on live coals, which are always formed from pecan twigs, to produce a thick aromatic smoke which is inhaled by patients suffering from ghost sickness, vertigo, or severe headache. The cedar smoke is also fanned over an individual by Sanapia in her blessing ceremony, a prominent aspect of all her doctoring activities. She uses the cedar medicine smoke in any instance when she is called upon to dispel the influences of the ghosts. When she is commissioned to ritually cleanse a house in which a death has recently occurred, she employs cedar smoke as a central core in this activity. When an individual is plagued by thoughts of a deceased relative, Sanapia prescribes a fumigation of the home with cedar smoke. She also strongly urges "cedaring" of the sleeping area before retiring at night.

Only use that red berry kind . . . get it on those slick hills west of here. They say when you use that cedar and they smell it, it blows all that bad stuff and pain away from you with that smoke. It keeps you well, and you won't ever be scared or nothing. Lot of different ways it help you like that. It's green, and its living all the time. In winter, summer, anytime. I don't care when. It's got Medicine for that. That's why I use it.

natsa^{n}ksi

"sneezing medicine"   *Helinium microcephalum*   (sneezeweed)

This plant is collected in the early fall. The flowers are detached and allowed to dry. When dried, the flowers are crushed and inhaled through the nose to produce the desired violent sneezing.

Sneezing medicine is administered to patients suffering from heart "flutter," low blood pressure, and head and nasal congestion. In Sanapia's opinion, the sneezing stimulated by this medicine keeps the heart beating steadily and strongly, thus maintaining the proper blood pressure. Also, she has the notion that in old age the heart becomes loosened from the cavity in which it is supposed to be housed. The violent sneezing caused by this medicine is capable of shocking the heart back into its proper position.

For those suffering from sinus congestion or head colds, Sanapia makes a very effective "inhaler" out of a small bottle or can. The container is half filled with the sneezing medicine. The patient is directed to shake the container, remove the lid, and inhale the dust when he is suffering from head congestion. Sanapia got the idea for her inhaler from commercials for cold remedies which she has seen on television. Many of her ideas concerning the nature of head and chest congestion and especially colds stem from notions absorbed from viewing television commercials. She uses terms like "bronmicha" for "bronchial" and "simus" for "sinus." The bronmicha is everything in the chest cavity except the lungs and heart. Her idea of the location of the sinus cavities is essentially correct, though she does not understand their function.

ekəpa

"red bean"   *Sophora secundiflora*   (mescal bean)

Sanapia grinds the mescal bean to the consistency of granulated sugar and then boils this coarse powder, which she first wraps in a makeshift cloth bag. When the decoction has reached the desired brownish coloration, it is strained through another piece of cloth, and the liquid is used as eardrops in the doctoring of earaches and sores deep in the ear. Sanapia reports that her maternal uncle, a *puhakut*, would sew mescal beans into the cuffs of his trousers as protection against possible contamination from menstrual blood.

puitsasene

"eye scraper"   *Elymus sp.*   (rye grass)

Sanapia uses a single looped blade of this grass as a filelike tool in the removing of "cataracts" (trichoma). She describes this treatment as follows:

You take that and double it up and turn the eye lid over and scrape it just as easy as you can. Then you just scrape it and scrape it until it bleeds . . . that thing on there bleeds. Well, you just keep on scraping until it finally comes off. Its the eye lid that causes cataracts because those things rub on the eye and make them sores. You got to scrape the eye. Put sugar water on it after you scrap it. It makes it feel better. Put sugar on after that thing stops bleeding.

kunənatsu

"fire medicine"   *Zanthoxylum americanum*   (prickly ash)

An infusion is made from the root of this plant and used for the treatment of fever. The powdered root is also used in the treatment of toothache and burns. For toothaches, the powder is wrapped in a piece of cloth and this tiny bundle of medicine is placed next to the afflicted tooth. The medicine promotes a numbing in the mouth. In the treatment of burns, the powder is sprinkled dry on the burn. The term "fire medicine" stems from the burning sensation which this medicine causes when it contacts an open wound.

bakuma^k

"in the water"   *Iris sp.*   (iris)

This plant is an unidentified variety of *Iris* which is not native to Sanapia's home area of Comanche County, Oklahoma. Sanapia utilizes a decoction of the root in the treatment of colds, upset stomache, and sore throat.

bakuma^k is the only medicine plant whose locale of growth is to some extent controlled by Sanapia. Her mother transplanted a number of these plants to a spring near Sanapia's home, and Sanapia makes an effort in her collection of this plant to never totally deplete the planting made by her mother.

This *Iris* is very similar to a variety which is found in eastern Oklahoma, significantly in an area of high Creek Indian population density. The Comanches and the Creeks have had close ties since the late nineteenth century (Wallace and Hoebel 1952:304), and Sanapia remembers traveling with her mother to eastern Oklahoma to visit Creek acquaintances. It is possible that Sanapia's mother could have learned of the medicinal qualities of this plant from the Creeks and brought back a collection to her home in Comanche County. The peculiar characteristics of the variety of *Iris* which Sanapia uses as medicine could have resulted from natural modifications stimulated through time by this change in environment.

pɔhɔβi

"white sage"   *Artemisia ludoviciana*   (lobed cudweed; gray sage)

Sanapia employs the leaves of the gray sage in treatment of insect and spider bites. She chews the leaves and rubs the resulting moist pulp over the area of bites to relieve itching and swelling.

ɛsipɔhɔβi

"sweet smelling sage"   *Poliomentha incana*   (sweet sage)

This medicine plant comes from the area of the Mescalero Apache reservation in southeastern New Mexico. It is obtained for Sanapia by Fort Sill Apaches who have ties with the Mescalero.

In a doctoring situation when Sanapia must apply her mouth to the afflicted area of the patient's body in an attempt to suck the sickness from the patient, she chews a small piece of sweet sage and retains it in her mouth with the masticated medicine which is being specifically employed at the time. She states that the sweet sage acts to sweeten the usually bitter taste which results from this type of procedure. Sweet sage, in certain circumstances, is also added to *bekwinatsu* (to be discussed) to increase its potency. It is also added to various medicinal "teas" to make them more palatable to the patients.

During Comanche peyote meetings held on Sanapia's property, it was pointed out that the leafy cushion upon which the Chief Peyote rested was made of sweet sage. The sweet sage used in the peyote meeting is particularly valued by Sanapia as a medicine since it gains an added potency through its contact with the Chief Peyote.

bekwinatsu

"swelling medicine"   *Matelea biflora* or *cynanchoides*   (recumbent milkweed)

This is one of Sanapia's major medicines and one of the three plants which she attributes with some degree of intrinsic supernatural potential. The other two medicines so considered are peyote and cedar.

A decoction of the thick white root is externally administered in the treatment of ghost sickness, bruises, bone breaks, and menstrual cramps. A paste made from the root is used to coat the finger during the treatment of "poking the throat." This procedure is usually initiated in the case of children with diphtheria or other conditions which are acting to close the throat passage. Sanapia applies the paste to her index finger and lightly probes the child's throat to the extent of her finger's reach. This same paste is used as a liniment in all cases of severe stomach pains. In addition, Sanapia spews from her mouth a very dilute decoction of this medicine on patients suffering from ghost sickness.

There is more ritual activity involved with the collection of *bekwinatsu* than with any other plant medicine which Sanapia utilizes. Upon approaching the area in which the plant will be collected, Sanapia recites a short prayer.

> Well, I tell it that I'm coming to take it way with me. I say that I need you help peoples that got twisted face . . . what them ghosts do to peoples, you know. Then I tell it that I'm going to give it something in return. I supposed to put a piece of green goods over its branche before I dig it out. Sometimes I do and sometimes I don't. Sometimes I'm in a hurry so I don't do that, but that's what I'm supposed to do, that's what my uncle told me to do.

When she approaches the plant, she situates herself to the west of the plant and drapes a small strip of dark green cloth over the spindly branches. She then digs the plant from the ground, detaches the long root, and deposits the remainder of the plant over the hole from which it was extracted with the strip of green cloth attached to one of the branches.

sanawiha

"yellow flowers"; "makes knife sticky"   *Guitierrezia dracunculoides* (broomweed)

Sanapia uses this plant medicine for the treatment of exzema and rashes when prepared as she describes.

> Get the tops . . . the flowers . . . and boil them into a jelly. Now, when anybody got excema, you just wrap it on . . . put it on a rag and wrap it on there. Use the tops . . . just tops. Boil them good and when they cool down, they get just like jelly. That jelly is what you use for medicine.

kusiwɜna

"it's gray"   [No specimen]

This is one of Sanapia's major medicines. It is used as an addition to many medicinal preparations to increase their potency. An infusion made from the root is also used as a sedative in the absence of peyote or concomitantly with peyote. It is specifically used, however, in the treatment of "fits" (epilepsy?) and as the main medicine employed in the treatment of witch victims.

When used to treat fits, the splintered root is boiled to a tea, and the patient is liberally dosed with this decoction until the symptoms subside. According to Sanapia, this root is unusually hard and therefore difficult to prepare for use as a medicine. However, she considers its extreme hardness as a positive quality since she associates hardness with compactness; therefore, she feels there is more medicine to a piece of *kusiw3na* than there would be to practically any other medicine of equal size.

In the treatment of victims of witchcraft, a decoction of this root is utilized in several different ways. It can be made into a thick paste which is applied to an area of minute incisions which are made by Sanapia with slivers of glass before she begins to suck from the victim the magically toxic feather which has been introduced into the victim's body by the witch. The decoction can also be drunk by the patient, or it can be spewed on him by Sanapia in the course of treatment.

do:ltsa

[No translation]   [No specimen]

Sanapia obtains this medicine from Shoshone friends who live on the Fort Washakie reservation in central Wyoming. She utilizes the thick root of this plant, without modification, as a medicine to induce appetite and stimulate weight gain. A decoction made from this root is also used in the treatment of tuberculosis.

From Sanapia's description of *do:ltsa* and its properties, it could be suggested that this plant is *Perideridia gairdneri*, a wild caraway, called *yap* by the Comanches (Kearney 1951:615). Since Sanapia first acquired this medicine from an Arapaho uncle, who in turn suggested to her certain Shoshone as further sources for it, the name which she uses may well be Arapaho, Shoshone, or Sanapia's Comanche-ized corruption of an Arapaho or Shoshone word which is applied to this plant.

bə:tasas

"looks like feathers"   [No specimen]

This medicine, like sweet sage, is obtained for Sanapia by Fort Sill Apaches from the Mescalero country. The fruiting body is made into an infusion which is internally administered in the treatment of tuberculosis, various stomach complaints, and postnatal hemorrhaging. A thick paste is prepared from these fruiting bodies and applied as a liniment to the chest and throat of those suffering from pneumonia. No specimen would be obtained. However, from Sanapia's description, *Agoseris* might be suggested as a highly probably genus affiliation.

oinatsu

"vomit medicine"   [No specimen]

Sanapia reports but one use for this medicine plant. A decoction of the root is taken internally by patients afflicted with asthma or chest congestion. The described results are quite spectacular.

You just give them a cup full of this, and another cup, and another, and another . . . they just be filled up with that medicine. Sit around for ten or fifteen minutes and that medicine just goes in their stomach and stirs up all that fluid, whatever it is. When you got asthma, you got all those bronmicha [sic] tubes filled with slobber. That medicine takes it out. It comes out by itself, you don't have to vomit or nothing . . . through the mouth . . . comes right out. Some of it comes through the nose too. It runs out fast and they get well. You don't have to treat them another day longer.

itse

[No translation]   [No specimen]

This medicine comes from the Mescalero Apache region and is obtained from the same sources which supply Sanapia with ba:tasas and εsipɔhɔβi. Dr. Harry W. Basehart of the University of New Mexico, who has done field research among the Mescalero, states the word itse is very similar to a Mescalero word which means "mystical influence." Mrs. Julia A. Jordon made a similar suggestion based on her experience with the Kiowa-Apache of Oklahoma. There is a strong possibility, then, that this word has been borrowed from Apache into Comanche.

The part of the plant which is utilized as medicine seems to be from Sanapia's description, a fruiting body. The plant is chiefly used as a remedy for the bites of rattlesnakes and as a rattlesnake repellent. Sanapia describes how she uses it as a snake repellent for her son:

When he goes to the field, like now, I have it boiled and I just rub it on his leg like that and then a cloth and pour it on and tie it around his boots . . . pour it all on there. Now if there's a rattlesnake running right there, he right up on him, but he won't jump him. He smells that and he just lay low. It'll kill that snake right now. I don't know how it does it. That medicine is really strong. A rattlesnake ain't going to smell it. They going to die if they smell it.

Sanapia recalls that she saw old people among the Comanche carry it in small cloth sacks tied to their belts or around their ankles in order to repel snakes. In the case of snake bite, the itse is chewed to a pulpy consistency and spread over the fang punctures, or it is retained in the mouth of the one who attempts to suck the poison from the wound. It is also used in this manner for the bites of poisonous spiders and scorpions.

In addition, Sanapia boils it into a thick broth for patients suffering from pneumonia. She notes that one of itse's interesting characteristics is that it causes excessive salivation, and she therefore employs it when she must induce salivation in a patient.

osidobeda

"peyote"   Lophophora williamsii (peyote)

Peyote is Sanapia's most utilized general medicine, and in her opinion its curative properties can aid in healing any type of human physical affliction. She grinds and pounds the dried buttons to a powder which is then boiled or steeped to produce a decoction or infusion of the desired consistency and coloration, or she employs the powdered peyote buttons alone. She also makes a medicinal relish from the green peyote buttons. In many cases the peyote is left unaltered and used in its dried or green state.

As mentioned, Sanapia can involve peyote in the treatment of any type of illness. Peyote is used mainly by Sanapia as a painkiller and sedative. It can be prepared in numerous ways. To quiet pain, Sanapia gives the patient four peyote buttons to eat, in most cases by chewing them first. For colds, pneumonia, and internal disorders, a decoction or infusion of peyote, commonly called "peyote tea," is administered.

When treating ghost sickness, Sanapia manipulates peyote in several ways. The patient is given four buttons to act as a sedative. During treatment Sanapia puts some dilute peyote tea in her mouth, releases a portion of it into her hands, and applies this to the affected portions of the patient's face. While retaining some of the solution in her mouth, she applies her mouth to the patient's face. She may also spew this thin decoction over the patient if she believes this type of procedure would be efficacious.

She applies thin, latitudinal, coinlike slices of the peyote button in the treatment of arthritis, severe headaches, heart pains, and in any relatively localized area of pain. Of course, a liquid preparation of peyote can also be administered in these conditions. The exact manner of administration and preparation of all medicines is determined by Sanapia through experience and inspiration.

Sanapia carries several peyote buttons with her at all times. She considers this her minimal doctoring kit. Peyote is extremely important to Sanapia as a medicine. However, she feels that her powers make her superior to the peyote. She states that peyote is the most powerful of all plant medicines. It is also one of the few medicines which Sanapia talks to and the only one which she threatens.

təpinatsu

"rock medicine"

This medicine is not a botanical item. I include it under the section on botanical medicines for several reasons. Sanapia feels that rock medicine is totally composed of plant parts. Also, at times she speaks of it "growing on rocks."

Təpinatsu is the word which Sanapia applies to the gummy, amber-colored matrix produced by a variety of mason bee as the basic material for its egg depositories. This solitary bee affixes these irregularly shaped cases, which are usually between ½ and 1 inch in diameter and approximately one-fourth of an inch thick, to rocks and then proceeds to camouflage the case by inserting local grains of sand and pieces of gravel into the sticky matrix of the case. It is from the resulting rocklike appearance that the medicine gains its Comanche name. Sanapia describes its composition:

Some little bitty bugs get gum from the cedars on them slick hills. Then they take bites from the yellow flowers on them broomweeds, and some sage too. Put it in their bodies and mix it up so they can stick it on these rocks like you can see. That's why this medicine works best with cedar.

Rock medicine is only used in conjunction with cedar: Both are deposited on live coals to produce medicine smoke. The *təpinatsu* sputters when placed on the coals and produces a thick white smoke which is not unlike cedar smoke in odor, though more pungent. This medicine's major use is in the treatment of ghost sickness and the results of witchcraft.

Sanapia picks the tiny pebbles and grains of sand from the *təpinatsu* and forms the then-translucent amber-colored gum into a ball about an inch in diameter. She rolls the ball between her palms and the heat and friction polish it to a glassy brown-gold color. It is in this form that it is utilized as medicine.

There is a medicine similar in kind to *təpinatsu* which Sanapia reports is found in the vicinity of Wichita Falls, Texas. The Comanche word for it, according to Sanapia, means "rats make it." It is described as being of the same composition as *təpinatsu*; however, instead of being produced by "little bugs," it is believed to be produced by pack rats. The gummy substance is melted in hot water, and persons suffering from paralysis, other than the kind caused by ghosts, are bathed in this concoction. This medicine, unmelted, is also applied directly to the area of paralysis. Sanapia remembers that her mother used this medicine; however, it was not transferred to Sanapia when she became a doctor.

Another medicine plant of which Sanapia has knowledge, but which was not transmitted by her mother to her, is one which, when mixed *bekwinatsu*, was administered as a sedative to women in protracted labor. The seeds of this plant were utilized as medicine when boiled into a medicinal decoction. Sanapia also states that the seeds of this plant augment the attractive aroma of Indian perfume (*Monarda fisulosa*) when the two are mixed and moistened.

I can just sit here and look at them bald prairies and see four kinds of medicines growing. I bet you can't even see them? Not many . . . even of my people, up to today, can even see them growing early in the spring. I can because I've learned that way. There's lots of plants that can get you well, but they ain't many people who even know that anymore.

4

Ghosts and Ghost Sickness

Comanche Attitudes toward Ghosts

WALLACE AND HOEBEL (1952:173) write concerning the Comanches' attitudes toward ghosts: "Ghosts did not generally bother the Comanches, but the Comanches were definitely uneasy about them." Kardiner (1945:84) states that the Comanches have no ghost fear at all. I found that not only did my older Comanche informants feel uneasy about ghosts but in most cases they were terrified by them. In almost every interview with a Comanche informant, some situation was cited that dealt with the horrors which ghosts are capable of afflicting on the living.

Sanapia states that the whirlwinds, or "dust devils," common in southern Oklahoma are the only form which the ghosts take which is entirely visible to the human eye. In addition this is the only form by which the ghost will make his presence known during daylight hours. The nocturnal guise of the ghost is probably humanlike, in Sanapia's opinion, though she states that she has never seen a ghost at night. This fact is irksome to her because she believes herself to be an expert on the matter of ghosts and their behavior among the Comanches. She considers the lack of this experience as a major flaw in her background, though she accounts for it by mentioning the fear which her Medicine inspires in ghosts. The following is her description of an attempt she made to meet a ghost:

> I tried it on a real dark night. I took my flashlight and walked from here to the highway. The darkest night. That's what I supposed to do because the ghost hates me and I hate it. He ain't never going to do nothing to me because I'm going to overpower that ghost. I could kill it, and the things that it done to a person. He won't do that to me because I got that Medicine. So I walk here to the highway the darkest night. They say there's ghost on the road, but I never did see any. I went to the highway, and then I come back. I just wanted to try. If there was a ghost, I never did hear one, I never see one. Nothing touch me, nothing in my way. I just wanted to see how it was for them to scare

65

a person . . . see how it is for it to scare me, but I didn't feel nothing. Nothing didn't scare me at all.

Sanapia feels that ghosts are probably the spirits of deceased persons who led evil lives and who are therefore doomed to wander the earth forever. Good people, according to Sanapia, probably go to the Christian heaven. She is not quite sure. Ghosts tend to remain near people and things which were familiar to them when they were alive. However, no particular correspondence between ghosts and certain deceased relatives exists. Ghosts are generally described as being "jealous hearted." They are jealous of the living.

Sometimes you be sleeping. They comes around and they just put something . . . dirt on your face. Or the whirlwind, they say that it is a ghost. It goes around and . . . supposing you be out there by yourself and here comes a whirlwind and just pass you like that. It don't often do that to anybody . . . just once in awhile it do that to somebody, and it twist their face. When I see them whirl-winds coming to me I say, "You go that way. Leave me alone," and it does it because I got that power. Or else sometimes people get scared when they laying in bed at night and one of those people of the family dies and the Indians say they get jealous of the one that are living in that house . . . either their sister or their son or their aunt or anything like that. They get jealous because they living and he died. And they the ones that come bother you like that. Some-times they come in and you hear them just walking. They open the door and come in and come to your bed and they jerk your covers off or either just pull your hair like that or hold your hand. That's when they do that to you . . . twist your face.

Sanapia is not consistent in her statements concerning belief in the existence of ghosts. She feels certain of the existence of some kind of malevolent spirit which causes ill effects to those human to which it appears, but she is not sure that these ghosts are actually the spirits of men who were once alive. The Cheyenne, for example, felt that ghosts were derived from the dead but that they were not related to a specific dead individual (Hoebel 1960:86). Perhaps Sanapia's relations in Cheyenne-Arapaho culture have caused her to be ambivalent on point. At one time she will state that ghosts are the spirits of the deceased who while alive led evil lives, and at other times she will make statements such as the following:

Some of them would hear noises in the dark and think they see things . . . ghosts. That's what they think. I just think its their imagination . . . that's what. Because when anybody dead, they're gone. They ain't going to come back. How can they?

Ghost Sickness

The particular horror of the ghost is his ability to deform his victims, usually by causing contortions of the facial muscles and in some instances paralysis of hands and arms. This condition is called "ghost sickness," or "twisted face," by

Sanapia. The Comanche name for ghost sickness is *bɛdɛɣai*, which Sanapia translates as "ghost done it." She describes the condition in this manner:

> You seen them, I guess. Their face get all twisted up on one way, and their
> eyes might get twisted up on the left side and their mouth would twist around
> too. Their eyes run all the time and they can't hardly see. You can see the
> gums in their mouth and the teeth. They get to slobbering so bad that they
> got to hold a rag over their mouth. Sometimes their hands get bent up and
> their arms get turned around and they be shaking sometimes. Oh! they stink
> when they get it, just like dead persons. I'll tell you, when you doctor someone
> with twisted face, its the most nasty thing you could do. You have to put your
> mouth right on it.

Usually, the ghosts do their harm to individuals whom they find outside
and alone at night. The following is an example, from a Comanche informant, of
a very standardized account of ghost contact. This tale, with only slight variations,
was also collected from Kiowa and Kiowa-Apache informants.

> We was up around Fletcher picking pecans one afternoon. It started getting
> late, but we didn't notice because we were having a good time. And the
> sun went down, so I told that bunch I was with that I was going. I started to
> walk to my pick-up parked up on the highway. And so I was walking. It was
> then that I heard something around me. Some sound like somebody walking
> behind me in the grass. The hair about to stand up on my head, because I
> knew what it was right then. So I start running. I run, and run, and run. After
> a time I turn my head to see if I loose it and, bang, it hit me right on this
> side of my face. It was right behind me every minute I was running. I fell down
> hard when it happened and seems like I went to sleep or something. When I
> woke up, it was still dark and my face was chilled-like, you know, it was dead
> feeling. So I got home after a while and my wife gave a holler when she see
> me with my face all screwed up like that. I guess it look pretty bad alright.
> Didn't hurt. It just look bad. We got it fixed up later. Indian doctor fix it up
> pretty good for me.

A key point to these tales of the appearance of the ghosts and the subsequent contortion of the face of the individual contacted lies in the emotion of
fear. In every tale of this nature, the ghost victim states the fear he felt at the
sight or sound of the ghost. I also collected several accounts in which the individual contacted by the ghost describes how he managed to control his fear at
the appearance of the ghost and thus avoided the ghost contortions. Sanapia is
very explicit on this point. She states that the only defense against the ghost is
courage.

> You might be walking along, out there someplace, and you hear some sound
> moving along behind you. If you going to turn around, you got to turn all
> around, turn your whole body around, and look right at it. See what it is. But
> if you just turn your head, take a peek, that's when they twist your face. Turn
> all the way around and look at it and say, "What do you want? Come here,
> let me see you," or "Go away. You're dead." Say that to it and it's gone. That's
> the way they do. You got to stand up to that ghost. You got to show it you
> ain't afraid of it. If you don't, they got you, and they twist you up right now.

Sanapia reports that ghost sickness is sometimes called "stroke" by white men. She makes a distinction between the two and will not attempt to doctor someone with a stroke, feeling that this affliction is a white man's disease and therefore the province of white doctors. Sanapia states that persons suffering from ghost sickness exude an offensive odor which is not present in the case of stroke. The ghost-sickness victim also possesses an aura of evil, detectable by Sanapia because of her special powers, which she cannot detect in a patient suffering from a stroke. The visible symptoms of the two can be very similar though. Further, certain effects of witchcraft can be almost identical to the symptomatic traits of ghost sickness; however, with witchcraft Sanapia reports that the victim's eyes do not water and he does not salivate excessively. Also, the contortions of the face and the contractions of the hands and arms usually appear in spasmodic cycles rather than as a relatively constant state of contorted paralysis as in ghost sickness.

Wallace and Hoebel (1952:174) make the following statement when discussing Comanche *puhakuts*: "Sorcery with ghost medicine is supposed to cause paralysis." As already mentioned, and as will be more fully discussed in Chapter 5, witching or sorcery by an eagle doctor, a doctor with ghost Medicine, not only causes paralysis but a type of paralysis almost identical to that which appears in ghost sickness. The conclusion seems to follow that a doctor with ghost Medicine, or power greater than ghosts, would have the ability to control the behavior of ghosts in any way that he wished, from dismissing them or their effects on living men to directing them to perform harmful acts to humans. Sanapia does not recognize the connection in the similarity in the symptom of ghost sickness and witch sickness, and she maintains that doctors with her particular powers are only able to cure the effects of the ghost's actions, but they are unable to affect the behavior of ghosts in any way, such as directing them to harm a specific individual.

Ghost Fear in the Basin and on the Plains

In discussing the roots of Comanche culture, it was noted that a lively ghost fear was present among the Basin-Range peoples. When the Comanches moved onto the Plains, this ghost fear apparently disappeared, or, at least its prevalence greatly diminished (Kardiner 1945:84; Wallace and Hoebel 1952: 173). However, my field research has shown that at present the more traditional Comanches possess a prominent ghost-fear complex. What factors can be suggested to explain the deemphasis of ghost fear in the Comanche transition from the Basin to the Plains, and how can its reappearance in twentieth-century Comanche society be accounted for?

Kardiner (1945:94) suggested that ghost fear, and possibly the prevalence of witchcraft, decreased in importance in the transition from Basin to Plains because the Plains Comanches were able to release aggressions and hostility outside the primary group through the institutionalized war complex. My model Basin culture possessed no patterns of warfare through which intrasocially spawned tensions and aggression could be released in such a way that the societal fabric would not be torn in the process. Because of the excessive rigors of the environment, emphasis was necessarily placed on cooperation and supportiveness among group members. Perhaps Basin culture ghost-fear beliefs acted as a means by which aggressive antisocial tendencies, stimulated in this potentially tension-ridden society, could be projected, displaced, or transferred outside the group, much as the Plains cultures could direct intragroup motivated anxiety outside the group and toward their enemies through the war complex. The Basin people, lacking warfare patterns and not being able to afford excessive intragroup aggressions or asocial behavior, were able to project their fears, anxieties, tensions, and so forth toward ghosts. This specific type of displacement target is especially effective since it exists outside the realm of living men. Ghosts inhabit another world or plane of existence. Ghosts, besides being something to hate, fear, and aggress against, can also serve to explain misfortune, illness, and those occurrences in life which possess no natural explanations. However, that the ghosts functioned mainly in Basin culture as a means of displacing intrasocially motivated aggressive impulses is strongly suggested by the effectiveness of the Comanche war complex in decreasing ghost fear. Other factors which were doubtless of significance in leading to a decrease in ghost fear among the nomadic Comanches were the highly mobile nature of Comanche society, the more favorable environment of the Plains, the ability to increase geographic distance between group members and bands, and the subsequent ability of the Comanche individual to acquire a greater degree of independence from his primary group.

The Resurgence of the Ghost Complex

The life style of the nomadic culture, as opposed to the Basin prototype, tended to place heavy emphasis on individual assertiveness, independence, aggressiveness, and physical prowess. These gross aspects of traditional Comanche personality are relevant in understanding the severity of personal and social-cultural tensions which occurred when, in the reservation and postreservation period, the Comanche individual was to a great extent denied the prerogative of expressing himself in the traditional Comanche manner. Simply stated, the dynamic, mobile, and assertive Comanche personality was suddenly penned and confined because it came in conflict with the dominant white society's concept of proper and acceptable personal expression. Traditional Comanche modes of personal expression were not only deemed of negative value by the white society but they were subject to punishment as well. Therefore, certain Comanche personality traits, perfectly acceptable and functional in a culture where aggression, for example, could be released at a distance from the group and with the group approval, were suddenly loosed within the group because of its sudden forced confinement. Add to this the emotionally defined cleavage in Comanche society based on differential acceptance rates of acculturation stimuli between bands, and the presence of a high degree of psychological and sociocultural anxiety and tension in contemporary Comanche society is understandable. The notion of ghosts and their ability to interfere in human affairs has found new vitality among twentieth-century Comanches as they attempt to discover alternative methods of expressing and relieving the potentially dysfunctional emotional states which now plague them.

A further suggestion that the ghost complex among the contemporary Comanches function to relieve intrasocial tensions which have appeared as a result of the myriad influences of the acculturation situation is found in the most recent ethnographic studies of the Comanche, which were obtained by the Santa Fe group in 1933. In all the materials published as a result of this group's work, the Comanches are not mentioned as possessing a great degree of ghost fear. This feature is very obviously present today, however. Since the Comanche "capture" occurred in the late nineteenth century, it can be assumed that a relatively large proportion of the Comanche population living in 1933, at the time of the Santa Fe group's investigation, would be composed of individuals who had actually taken part in the nomandic Comanche culture. The influence of this select group on the Comanche society of the 1930s was no doubt great. Their presence probably served to prolong the existence of traditional values and world view in vital form well into the postreservation-period Comanche generation; this would include the relative absence of ghost fear. At present, however, the majority of Comanches are two to four generations removed from the time of the nomadic Comanche culture, and it is among these people that the ghost complex has found new life and meaning. If the material collected by the 1933 group is indeed correct, it would appear that Comanche's attitudes toward ghosts have developed to their present form only since the 1930s. Sanapia has volunteered the information that the incidences of ghost sickness among the Comanche have been increasing over the last thirty years.

Some of the specific social forces which have been active in Comanche society within this time span and which have no doubt contributed to the resurgence in ghost belief have already been suggested. Conflict between the values of the white and Comanche society, increased intrasocial tensions in Comanche society, and lack of a satisfactory means to displace aggressive socially disruptive forces away from the society must be counted as three major forces toward disequilibrium in Comanche society. To this list can be added racial discrimination and prejudice on the part of white society and to a certain extent on the part of Comanches. Associated with these aspects are the increasing pressures toward assimilation of the Comanche society being exercised by white society. However, while the Comanches are being persuaded that the rewards of the white life style are more desirable than those of Comanche culture, they are in most cases denied the avenues to achieve these rewards. Through all of this, the gap between core traditional Comanche values and the extinct culture upon which these values are based continue to expand, leaving many Comanches in a limbo of apathy, ambivalence, and neurotic marginality.

The contemporary Comanche's belief in ghosts serves to relieve disruptive intrasocial tensions by presenting the members of this society with a means of directing frustrations, hostility, and other emotions of a potentially dysfunctional nature, both to the individual and the group, toward a target outside the culture's boundaries. It is also significant that ghosts are outside the boundaries of white society. Therefore the dangers of aggressing toward a source which could effectively retaliate is lessened. Although witch fear serves this same function in some cultures, the particular nature of Comanche witchcraft beliefs precludes its similar use in Comanche society. In Comanche society witchcraft is usually worked by *puhakuts*. Therefore, the individual who may have witched your uncle last month may be the only one who could cure you if you contracted ghost sickness tomorrow.

Debt to the Kiowa and Kiowa-Apache

It appears very likely that the Comanches borrowed heavily from their Kiowa and Kiowa-Apache neighbor's ghost beliefs to revitalize and supplement their own ghost complex. Possibly, the Comanche ghost complex lost much in complexity and elaboration during the many decades of its relative insignificance among the nomadic Comanches. The contemporary Comanche, Kiowa, and Kiowa-Apache notions of ghosts, their nature, and their effects on the living are very similar in general design. However, Kiowa and Kiowa-Apache ghost beliefs, relative to the Comanche's, seem to be much more systematic, consistent, and elaborated. This view is substantiated by a perusal of some of the relevant field notes of others who have done research among these peoples (Bittle 1967; Freeman 1968). Sanapia's use of a crow feather amulet against ghosts can be presented as a specific example. Sanapia and several other Comanche informants, though feeling that crow feathers act to repel ghosts, could offer no explanation for this peculiar property of the crow feathers. Kiowa and Kiowa-Apache informants, however, were quick to point out that the crow is the natural enemy of the owl, a standard guise of the ghosts. Therefore, crow feathers are magically used to enlist the aid of the crow against the owl. Comanches do not generally hold this notion of the association of the owl with ghosts, though they value crow feathers as protective amulets against ghosts. It appears that the Comanches borrowed the crow feather amulet without borrowing the rationale for its use.

Habits of Ghosts

Comanche ghost notions are uncomplicated. The following themes appear consistently in the accounts of actual ghost contact, though not so consistently in the idealized ghost lore. The Comanches have defined the ghost's operating hours to that time between sunset and sunrise and its area of operation in the majority of cases to any place that is relatively isolated. Though the ghost can appear during the daylight hours as a whirlwind, I collected no accounts of ghost sickness being contracted during that time. Cedar smoke or cedar leaves serve the Comanches as a totally effective ghost repellent. Thus, it seems that it would be a simple matter to avoid the ghosts: Keep a supply of cedar leaves in your house, and do not wander abroad at night in an isolated area unaccompanied. Yet

Comanches still incur ghost sickness and under conditions which they could have voluntarily avoided, conditions in which their culture assures them the ghost will be found. This strongly suggests the possibility that a Comanche may at some period in his life develop the need or desire to contract ghost sickness.

Preliminaries to the Treatment of Ghost Sickness

When an individual has contracted ghost sickness and has decided to seek Sanapia's aid in alleviating his distress, he first commissions an intermediary to arrange the initial interview between Sanapia and himself. This step can also be taken by the spouse of a patient. Since Sanapia is an older woman, the liaison should also be an older woman. The preferred intermediary would be a woman who had grown up with Sanapia, for they would be acquainted, would be of the same age and sex, and generally would have the same background. The potential patient pays the older woman to "speak for him." The payment is usually made in money.

The older woman approaches Sanapia with the afflicted person's request for treatment. This meeting is very informal and does not appear to be bound with any ritual behavior. The liaison discovers if Sanapia is accessible, when she would consent to meet with the patient, what kind of payment she would require, and if there are any specific kinds of behavior which Sanapia would require of the patient. It does not follow that a woman who has known Sanapia for a number of years would be able to know the answers to these questions simply from previous experience with Sanapia. Sanapia's accessibility depends on her schedule or proposed activities, as does the time when she would meet with the patient. Although the payment of a doctor is standardized to a degree, Sanapia will perhaps broadly suggest to the liaison that there is something which she needs and which would be readily acceptable as payment. Her opinion of the required deportment of the patient may change as her moods change, or perhaps as a result of a "real dream."

The importance of the liaison is stressed by informants who have been Sanapia's patients. Sanapia does not consider the liaison necessary, though she admits that she likes to know something about the person before he approaches her as a patient. The impression received from interviews with most informants who have been Sanapia's patients was that they really did not know exactly what was demanded of them when they desired to contract the services of a Medicine woman. The liaison also functions as the advisor on the deportment demanded of the patient by a Medicine woman.

When the first interview has been arranged and the patient is preparing to visit Sanapia, he makes a point to dress humbly. No jewelry is worn. His clothing should, by its poorness, add to the pitiable and humble image he wishes to present to Sanapia. He also must follow this theme in his conversation with Sanapia. The patient must act the part of the pitiable supplicant who is throwing himself on Sanapia's mercy and good graces. This is the standard posture utilized in prayers,

Ritual payment: four corn shucks, Bull Durham tobacco, and green cloth.

and in situations in which one individual must make a major request of another. By demeaning yourself to another, you are, in effect, pressuring him to acquiesce to your wishes; for by the Comanche code of generosity if he refused a request presented in such a fashion, he would indeed be a despicable person. A doctor who refused such an approach would be judged even more harshly by his community and his Medicine, for he has made an oath to uphold this code. This type of behavior on the part of the prospective patient acts as a normative pressure in the patient's attempt to contract Sanapia's services.

The formal contract occurs when the patient initiates the ritual involved with his request for Sanapia's aid. The short period of time which passes between the patient's appearance before Sanapia and the beginning of his ritual approach is described by Sanapia as follows:

> He might come here to my house, maybe somewhere else where I'm staying. "Do you know why I'm here?" I tell him, "Yeah. I guess I know why you come to see me." He be looking down at the floor and talking in a pitiful way. I just be sitting there and don't say nothing at first. I know why he's there and I just sit down and wait for him to say what he's got to say . . . just be sitting there quiet. I be watching him all the time.

The patient then produces the demanded items of payment which he has been instructed to bring by his liaison–advisor. This approach ritual payment consists of a piece of dark green cloth, a commercially obtained ⅝-ounce bag of Bull Durham tobacco, and four corn shuck cigarette "papers." The patient rolls a cigarette, takes four puffs, and hands the cigarette to Sanapia. When she takes it, the contract is made. Wallace and Hoebel state: "It is true that the Comanches smoked for pleasure, but never casually; and when smoking ceremonially, it was an oath, a signature to an agreement, a pledge on the part of the smoker" (1952: 180). After Sanapia has taken the cigarette, thus agreeing to the contract, the patient places the green cloth in front of her and lays the Bull Durham and the corn shuck leaves on the cloth.

Sanapia states that the requirement of the piece of dark green cloth follows from the nature of the major medicine which she employs in the treatment of ghost sickness. This type of payment can no doubt be connected with the ritual involved in her collection of *bekwinatsu*, or "swelling medicine." It is necessary for Sanapia to pay the plant with a piece of green cloth before extracting it from the earth.

> The medicine I use, that swelling medicine, got green leaves. The cloth goes with that. That's what the meaning of the dark green goods supposed to be. It stand for that, you might say. That kind of medicine get them well and they paying for it.

When Sanapia has accepted the cigarettte and taken the required four puffs, she says to the patient, "Tell me your troubles." The patient then begins to inform Sanapia of the specific reasons that he has sought her aid and generally to unburden himself concerning any and all varieties of "trouble" which he is experiencing. According to Sanapia, this patient monologue can continue for several hours. It is during this outpouring that Sanapia makes her diagnosis or decides exactly what course of action she will pursue regarding the patient.

Sanapia's doctoring ethics forbid her to divulge anything about which a patient has spoken to her. Many of Sanapia's expatients were aware of this fact or were advised of it by their liaisons, and they mentioned "how good it was to talk to that old lady." The patient has a rare opportunity to speak to an old and therefore, it is assumed, wise woman and to know that her supernatural sanctions forbid her to repeat anything she has been told. They are able to gain the counsel of a woman who has had many years experience in listening to these confidential disclosures. The patient also knows that because of the nature of the doctor–patient relationship, Sanapia will only pity him and offer sympathy. It would be considered impolite and improper if Sanapia censured her patient for anything he might say during his monologue.

> What they tell me I ain't supposed to tell anybody. It is so sad sometimes to listen to them. They say horrible things sometimes, but I guess that's because they sick peoples. But they come here and I can get them well. I've helped many people that way.

The psychotherapeutic tenor of Sanapia's doctoring is illustrated by the fact that she bases her diagnosis upon the nature of the emotional ventilation of the patient during his rambling monologue. She does not recognize that she bases her diagnosis on the content of the patient's disclosures but only that she makes her diagnosis after this occurrence. However, it is obvious from the material which has been presented and the material still to be presented that Sanapia is very aware of the psychological factor in illness and the necessity of treating psychological as well as physiological symptoms in a patient.

Treatment of Ghost Sickness

Immediately after this first interview, Sanapia instructs the patient to bathe in the stream which flows west of her house and to change his clothes. The actual treatment will begin after sunrise on the day following the first interview. Between this time and the time of the initiation of treatment, the patient is treated as a guest of Sanapia's household. During this time Sanapia sharpens her first diagnosis by a more thorough examination of the patient. Continual bathing is the only activity which is required of the patient. Since Sanapia will have to apply her mouth to the patient in her doctoring, she instructs him to wash often so he will be as clean as possible when Sanapia begins treatment. The notion of the magical effect of water is also probably present, though Sanapia never directly alluded to this.

Sanapia will doctor her patient three times daily for a period of two days. The treatment will be given at sunrise, midday, and sunset. By the morning of the third day the patient should be cured. Sanapia then blesses him, and the patient is dismissed. If, by the morning of the third day, the patient is not well, Sanapia continues her doctoring through another series of six treatments. After four days if the patient shows no sign of improvement, Sanapia will concede that she has failed in her attempts to cure her patient and will suggest either that he go to the white doctors in Lawton to obtain any comfort which they can supply or that he resign himself to his impending death. However, Sanapia states that even if she knows that her patient is going to die, she will usually not tell him because, as she says, "I can't stand to look at them when I have to say that to them. It makes me feel just so bad that I can't do it." Sanapia's ability to foretell the death of a patient is not solely based on her developed skills at prognosticating from the individual's physical condition. She states that she hears a voice which tells her that absolutely nothing can be done to save her patient.

I hear, "He's dead right now, he's dead right now." And I know they going to die. I know that part too. They would get up and sit up and talk and walk. Well, they eat their food and drink water and they feel good. But I know that's the last meal they going to have. That's the last drink they going to have.

Before sunrise on the day that she will begin treatment and before she awakens her patient, Sanapia selects and prepares the medicines she will use. She then ties them in a cloth bundle, for she will take them with her when she, accompanied by her patient, goes to make her prayers with the rising sun. She then awakens her patient, prepares his breakfast, and takes him to a secluded place on a small knoll south of her house. It is still dark when they walk to the selected place of prayer. Sanapia sits facing east with her patient beside her. She then unwraps her medicines and exposes them on the cloth in which they were wrapped.

Both Sanapia and her patient smoke Bull Durham tobacco wrapped in corn shucks as they wait for the sun to rise. Sanapia prays to the earth immediately before sunrise, and when the sun appears, she directs her prayers to it.

In the morning, before the sun come up, you go out away from the house, where nobody can hear you and you pray. You touch the ground with your hands, four times, and say . . . I don't know where it came from, but you say, "Mother earth, I want you to take my words. I want you to do what I want. I'm walking over you. I live on you, and I love you because you're my land." Say things like that to it. That sun not up yet. But it's the big eagle . . . talk to it like it's eagle . . . think of it like that, you know. It's going to fly up pretty soon when the sun comes up, and that's the eagle going to do everything I want.

The sun and the earth were the two greatest sources of power in the nomadic Comanche culture. Wallace and Hoebel (1952:190) write that ". . . only the sun, moon, and earth were looked upon as semi-dieties." They were also personified and addressed in prayer. The earth was considered second only to the sun in supernatural importance by the Comanches; however, though they were active in the affairs of men, neither the sun nor the earth gave personal power (Wallace and Hoebel 1952:195–197). Also in the content of the pages just cited are numerous mentions of the earth being addressed as "mother" by the Comanches. Kardiner (1945:63), when discussing Comanche beliefs associated with magic and power, writes: "The greatest powers were the earth, and the sun, with which the eagle was felt to be associated."

When the sun appears over the horizon, Sanapia begins her prayers in which she will ask "the eagle" to aid her in healing her patient. The patient, seated beside her, is instructed to pray for his recovery and to put his faith and trust in the powers of the earth and sun. She also indicates her medicines, exposed to the sun, and asks that it will fill them with power.

This period of prayer, first to the earth and then to the rising sun, lasts about half an hour, or until the sun has completely cleared the horizon. Sanapia then takes her patient back to her house, where her hubsnd or son have already prepared the pecan wood coals which Sanapia will need when she begins to doctor. Pecan coals are desired because they form long-burning, even coals. At this time she will attach her crow feather amulet to a beam on her front porch. She sometimes affixes several crow feathers to her patient's wrist.

As mentioned previously, in doctoring, Sanapia is alone with her patient. If she is in a tent or tepee, she sits on the south side of the tent, which is customarily facing east, and positions her patient directly in front of her. He lies on his back with his head toward the west. The medicines she will use are placed to her right, and the pecan coals are placed in an iron kettle or shovel so their position can be changed as Sanapia doctors. When she is in a house, she attempts to duplicate these conditions as closely as possible.

After her patient is situated, Sanapia begins her attempt to mobilize her various power sources for the task at hand. She deposits some cedar on the coals and smokes her Medicine feather by lightly waving it through the rising smoke four times. She then lays her feather on the fragment of Mexican sarape, which also underlies the medicines she will use, and holds her hands in the medicine smoke. With a washing motion, she draws the smoke over her face, arms, chest, and legs. After she "cleanses" herself with the smoke, she takes her feather and ceremonially fans her patient.

She then takes her Bible between her palms and, extending her arms before her, she prays to "God and Jesus and especially the Holy Ghost" to assist her in healing her patient. If she is inspired to do so, she will sometimes open her Bible at random and read from it in an attempt to receive a sign from "God, Jesus, or the Holy Ghost" concerning the direction she should take in her doctoring, or the possible outcome of her treatment.

Next, Sanapia picks up her Chief Peyote, and holding it in her right hand, she speaks to it. As mentioned in the chapter on medicines, Sanapia will usually threaten the peyote rather than beseech it or pray to it when she uses it in dotcoring. As she talks to it, she will transfer it from hand to hand in order to draw the power it possesses into her hands.

After Sanapia has made her opening prayers, she is in a very agitated emotional condition. This is mentioned both by Sanapia and by some of her expatients. She considers the chills, shaking, and trembling that she experiences as signs that her power has entered her, and she will not begin to doctor until she reaches this state.

And when I pray like that . . . well, that power just come over me, comes down and gives me that chills and I start shaking all at once and pretty soon it goes away and then I start. Sometimes I can't hardly touch them, the way my hand be shaking. It makes me feel like that power wants to make me get them well right now.

When she has regained control of her hands after the siege of trembling, Sanapia begins the treatment proper. She takes a segment of the white root of *bekwinatsu* and masticates it to a moist pulp. She then spews it over the patient's face, head, and arms if they have been affected by the ghost contagion. She also takes this moist pulp, and, after rolling it between her palms, she rubs it over the areas of the patient's body which exhibit symptoms of ghost sickness. After so doing, she deposits this premasticated root in the patient's mouth and instructs him to to swallow it.

Sanapia then chews another piece of *bekwinatsu* together with a few leaves of sweet sage to sweeten her mouth and, retaining this concoction in her mouth, applies her mouth to the contorted areas of the patient's face to suck out the sickness. Although she has the option of utilizing her sucking horn in other cases, she is obliged to use her mouth in the doctoring of ghost sickness.

Her mouth and hands are the areas of her body which are believed to be especially charged with power. This is the rationale for the spewing of medicines on a patient, the administering of medicines which have been premasticated by

Sanapia, Sanapia's handling of the medicines before she applies them to her patient, and the need of the direct application of the doctor's mouth in the treatment of ghost sickness, the most tenacious sickness Sanapia encounters.

When Sanapia turns her attention to the patient's twisted hands, a contortion which occurs in most cases of ghost sickness reported by Sanapia, her behavior and "bedside manner" undergo a radical change—from intensity and outwardly appearing agitation to gentleness and calm. She puts cedar and rock medicine on the coals to produce medicine smoke and then, manipulating the patient's hand, holds it over the rising smoke. During this phase of treatment she croons and sings to the patient and assures him that her powers will enable him to recover. She will also, at times, drape a black kerchief or a towel on the patient's face as she fans the medicine smoke over his face. After the smoking of the hand, she smooths it with her Medicine feather while her crooning tone is continued.

When her treatment of any afflicted extremity is completed, Sanapia once again places cedar and rock medicine on the coals and fans the medicine smoke over the patient. She then smokes the Medicine feather and draws the smoke over herself with a washing motion of her hands. At this point the first treatment is terminated.

The patient is instructed to rest after this first treatment. Sanapia rewraps her medicines before leaving the room in which she has been doctoring. She then immediately washes her hands and rinses her mouth with a commercial brand of mouth wash in order to destroy any "poison" which she feels may be in her mouth.

Between treatments the patient is continually dosed with a decoction of *bekwinatsu*. There are no dietary restrictions placed on him during his two-day treatment. Sanapia instructs her patient to rest, pray, and think only pleasant thoughts between treatments. During the midmorning and midafternoon when Sanapia is not involved in doctoring, she busies herself with her household chores and observes no special type of behavior connected with her doctoring. She does insist on decorum and a general quiet among household members during the several days of treatment for the sake of her patient.

When the sun reaches its zenith at midday, the second treatment is begun. This treatment will be similar to the morning treatment. By the end of the second treatment Sanapia will be able to determine if the patient is responding favorably. If the prognosis is good at this point, the subsequent treatments will all be similiar to the first one. However, if the patient is showing no sign of improvement or is worsening, Sanapia will begin to add more elements to her basic pattern of treatment. She will also be more susceptible to inspired variations since she believes that when her powers are with her to their fullest potential, any thoughts she has are of the order of a supernatural directive.

Use of the Peyote Meeting

If she feels that a crisis is developing with respect to her patient's condition, she will take her first step to augment the intensity of treatment during the third treatment at sunset on the first day. Sanapia will usually organize a specialized peyote meeting at this juncture. She carefully selects those to be invited, choosing only three or four individuals who she believes are especially good people and who have prayed with her in the past in similar situations. The local peyote leader is always included in this group since Sanapia concedes that it is his right to lead the meeting, though it is understood that it will be led for her purposes.

This meeting is held indoors. The fire is laid on a piece of sheet metal supported on several bricks. Most of the standard elements of a Comanche peyote meeting are present in this meeting—water drum, gourd rattles, sage wand, cedar staff, Chief Peyote, feather fans, eagle feathers, and Bull Durham tobacco and corn shucks for ceremonial smoking. The tepee is obviously lacking, as is the crescent-shaped earthen altar, the leader's whistle, the water ceremonies, and the ceremonial breakfast.

The meeting proceeds in the usual manner. Sanapia doctors throughout the meeting at those times when she feels particularly inspired to do so. When she desires to doctor, the leader signals those present to cease the singing and passing of the drum and accompanying paraphernalia. Sanapia then waits for the fire to die down to coals before she begins to doctor. She bases her treatment during the meeting on the basic pattern which she followed in the first two treatments earlier that day. However, at this time she adds the use of peyote to her doctoring.

After the smoking of her Medicine feather and herself, the fanning and smoking of her patient and all those present, and the applying of *bekwinatsu* she gives the patient four peyote buttons which she first has masticated. After the patient has taken the required first four buttons, he is doctored with a decoction of peyote. This "tea" is drunk by the patient, and it is applied externally by Sanapia as well as being spewed over the patient's face, head, and hands.

At sunrise when the meeting ends and the peyote drum is disassembled, Sanapia sometimes requests the moist drumhead from the leader and utilizes it in doctoring her patient. She presses the wet hide over the top of the patient's head and forms the hide to the contours of the patient's face while she prays that the patient's face will be cured when she takes the hide off. There is the notion that the pliable qualities of the wet hide will be transferred to the patient's face, and as Sanapia forms the hide, so might she reform the patient's contorted countenance.

She takes some of the sweet sage used to support the Chief Peyote used during the meeting, and after chewing it and rolling it between her hands, she rubs it over the afflicted areas of the patient's body. Sanapia takes a mouthful of water from the peyote drum and blows it over her patient. Some of the charcoal from the drum is used by Sanapia to draw a series of concentric circles on the contorted area of the patient's face. This magical act is supposed to constrict the "foamy stuff" which is causing the contortions of the face by first drawing it within the outer circle, then within the next smaller circle, and so on until the sickness is so localized that it will be a simple task for Sanapia to suck it out.

The seven stone "bosses" which are employed to attach the drum head to the kettle drum body are also utilized by Sanapia as medicine. Sanapia takes several in each hand and taps the patient's face. This is felt to transfer the positive qualities of these stones—firmness and stability—to the patient's face.

Intercession of the Medicine Eagle

If the patient is still not improved after the peyote meeting, Sanapia will move to her ultimate level of doctoring intensity by attempting to call her Medicine eagle to her assistance through the intercession of the spirits of her mother and maternal uncle. This step is not taken at the beginning of treatment because of the dangers involved with the presence of so great an amount of supernatural power. It is possible that she might kill her patient by exposing him to this burst of supernatural energy. Also, Sanapia forestalls calling her ultimate powers into play because of her feeling that the physical reactions which this powerful presence produces in her will ultimately cause her death.

On the second day, if she has decided to follow this course of action, she refrains from her sunrise and midday doctoring. The patient spends the day resting and drinking great quantities of peyote and *bekwinatsu* "tea." Sanapia passes the daylight hours alone in some secluded area preparing herself for the traumatic activities in which she will be engaged after sunset.

I set somewhere out there away from peoples . . . be by myself. I don't do nothing but sit and think about things. Like what my mother told me about things, and what my uncle told me. Think about all the years I come along and how up to today I'm still living. I don't do anything different from what I do if I am sitting anywhere by myself . . . just thinking about them things.

Immediately before sunset Sanapia goes to the stream which flows near her house and washes her hands and face before returning to her house. Any small children or infants who happen to be members of the household at this time are taken to spend the night with relatives in a nearby town, so they need not be exposed to the potential dangers of the night's doctoring activities. Sanapia firmly instructs her patient that he must do whatever she requests of him during the coming night. If he reacts slowly to her commands, he could die. Once again, this instruction is given in recognition of the dangers of supernatural power.

The night's doctoring follows the basic pattern of the first two treatments of the first day; however, this last treatment of the second day will continue throughout the night and will contain the crucial element of Sanapia's singing of her Medicine song. Sometime late in the night when Sanapia feels the proper inspiration, she begins to sing her song. She will sing it over and over again until the spirits she is calling come to her. The first singing of the song takes place with her patient as she fans him with her Medicine feather. She then leaves the house and continues her singing as she sits alone in the dark.

Sanapia first sees the spirits of her mother and uncle as two lights burning on the crest of a hill approximately a hundred yards south of her house. They slowly approach her. The rapidity of their approach corresponds to the intensity of Sanapia's singing, for it is her song which is drawing them to her. They finally stand before her, looking entirely natural and lifelike, much as they looked during Sanapia's adolescence. Sanapia continues her singing as they stand silently before her. In her song she tells them that she is alone and helpless and that she has no one to whom she can turn for help but them. She reminds them of their pledge of aid whenever she might need it during her lifetime. Sanapia may have to repeat her song for several hours as the spirits stand gazing down at her. Finally, with gestures of the hands they indicate that Sanapia will have what she wishes.

This means that the spirits of her mother and uncle have interceded with the Medicine eagle on her behalf. If the Medicine eagle is going to appear to Sanapia, it is at this time that he makes his appearance. Sanapia does not move after the spirits of her mother and uncle have left her. She ceases her Medicine song, but she remains to pray for a while longer before returning to her patient. Sanapia also must rest while her heart and breathing recover normalcy after the agitation they experienced during the apparition of the spirits.

She describes the appearance of the Medicine eagle in the following account:

I was so tired then and I was crying too. Sitting there and seeing my mother like that. All at once I felt cold wind pushing me down. It was on my head and all around . . . flatten down the grass around me and I had to lean on my hands because it was heavy like I thought it might push me down right over my face. My blanket was blowing off me and I was grabbing for it . . . blowing my hair all over. Got scared and started shaking. Boy! that wind blow dust in my eyes and I was rubbing them when all at once everything got calm . . . like a dream like when you be sleeping way in the night. I saw that eagle . . . big, big, like an eagle . . . shining so pretty on its feathers. And I guess I was being silly because I start crying some more . . . just like some old woman. But I hear it in my mind, you know, say, "Go ahead, get him well. You can do it." Then I don't see nothing . . . I guess it's gone then.

Sanapia returns to her patient and attempts to utilize her newly acquired power increase to cure him. She uses only her Medicine feather and medicine smoke at this point. Most of her energy is aimed at instilling in her patient, through her prayers and contact with her feather, enough power to negate the malevolent forces which are acting to keep the patient from recovering. She does not come in physical contact with the patient at this time, for she feels that such contact would kill him.

If her patient has recovered during the night, she takes him outside with her before sunrise to make her morning prayers. She then blesses him in the standard manner and instructs him to wear the red paint for two days before he washes it off. This blessing on the morning of the third day after the initiation of doctoring marks the end of treatment.

Payments

The final payment is made within the succeeding weeks. Sanapia does not state a price but must accept whatever is offered her. She has received from

$25 to $100 for her services as a doctor. The normal payment consists of about $30, plus groceries and enough cloth for several dresses. Several informants stated that the gift of groceries is connected with a belief that Sanapia eats the sickness which a patient might have; therefore, she should be given something good to eat as payment.

Sanapia's many comments concerning the difficulty of being a doctor often deal with the question of payments.

> Some people don't pay. They have to but they don't. They say, "Well, we haven't got no money now, but when we got money we'll pay you." They don't do it. My husband got to talking about it with some people that came here once. I was in there listening. He said, "Lots of people come here, and they come in real sick, real sick. She takes her time and doctor them, and she wait on them, and she even cook for them and give them eats because its two or three days before she get through with them. They promise her this and that and they never give it to her." There's many people that owe me that. I get tired, you know. Lots of times it get so hot in there doctoring them . . . sweating and tired out by the time I get through. And then I go through all that work for nothing.

The Necessity of Faith

An emergency situation sometimes arises when Sanapia must leave her house and go to the patient to doctor him. In this instance all of the formal first interview rituals are ignored, and Sanapia may begin doctoring with an intensity greater than that which she would be prone to initiate in an ordinary case. Sanapia customarily makes the following statement to those who appear at her home and hurriedly insist that she come at once to doctor a sick relative: "If I catch you between here and you alls place, they ain't no use in me doctoring." In other words, if Sanapia, leaving after the petitioners, overtakes them before they reach home where the sick individual lies, it signifies to Sanapia that the petitioners either do not care very much for the sick individual since they did not hurry back to him or they do not believe in Sanapia's powers. Sanapia's customarily made statement in this situation is involved with her feeling of the necessity of men's faith in power if they desire supernatural power to operate on their behalf.

Throughout the doctoring procedure, Sanapia continually prods the patient to have faith in her powers and the powers of the sun, earth, God, peyote, Jesus, Medicine eagle, and the Holy Ghost. It can also be remembered that many of the rituals involved with Sanapia's acquisition of power from her mother were colored by tests of faith and courage. Sanapia will admit that a person who does not believe in her power cannot be doctored by her: Her doctoring will have no effect. Also, a person who does not believe in ghosts and witches cannot be harmed by them. Wallace and Hoebel (1952:159) mention that the Comanches felt that if a *puhakut* did not believe in the powers he possessed, his powers would not work for him.

In order to instill this crucial element of faith in her patient, Sanapia admits that she does exaggerate her doctoring performance at times. She did not elaborate on this statement, only suggesting that she works to make her patient believe in her since he will not regain his health if he does not have faith in her powers. Some of Sanapia's expatients have noted her ability to make things appear and disappear; however, as mentioned previously, Sanapia will deny that she does sleight of hand.

Sanapia is aware that her shamanistic performance is expected by her patients and that it is a necessary element in strengthening their faith in her. However, she states that she could marshal her powers for healing without the performance, though the patient would not be highly impressed. Sanapia must move the patient to an emotional acceptance of her powers, for she feels that without the patient's confirmed faith her powers can do nothing toward curing him. Sanapia's belief that the patient's attitude toward the doctor is of significant importance in determining the outcome of the treatment is based in a sound grasp of psychotherapeutic principle, though in her case it is couched in the mystique of the faith healer.

Number of Patients per Year

How many patients does Sanapia doctor each year? This would be a difficult question to answer exactly. Sanapia does not think in these terms. Further she does not consider it "proper" to discuss the question. I would estimate, however, that she doctors approximately six cases of ghost sickness per year, and she may treat twenty patients suffering from more standard ailments during the same time. These estimates are based on clues collected during several years of interviewing and on observations of the contents of her medicine kit. I observed her medicine kit in the early fall when her medicines were almost totally depleted and watched as she collected what she felt would be a sufficient quantity of medicines to last until the next collecting season the following fall. From a knowledge of the possible combinations and quantities of dosages of these medicines, I estimated how many patients could be treated before the medicine supply would be depleted. This estimate corresponded closely with the estimates based on interview material.

What Is Ghost Sickness?

This is an important question. The key to understanding Sanapia's vital function in twentieth-century Comanche society rests with the answer. Ghost sickness may be an entirely organic or static affliction, perhaps a variety of organically motivated transient paralysis. Then again, a viewpoint suggesting the psychogenic nature of ghost sickness presented itself when Sanapia's accounts of ghost sickness victims were perused, particularly noting the age and sex of the victim. In the majority of cases, the victim was male, twenty-five to forty years of age. Also, based on interviews with ghost-sickness victims and information gathered from Comanche informants, it was discovered that these individuals were all very similar personalities.

The Comanches use "crooked mouth," "twisted face," and "twisted up" as synonyms for ghost sickness, and these terms are helpful in their descriptive capacity. It is also significant that Sanapia is almost always successful in curing this affliction in adults, though she is much less efficient in curing these same symptoms when they appear in infants and are considered the result of witchcraft.

A survey of the literature on hemiplegic disorders strongly suggests for consideration a vaguely understood variety of paralysis called Bell's palsy. Bell's palsy is due to the paralysis of the seventh cranial nerve and results in the paralysis of one-half the face. The condition is usually abrupt in onset, reaching its peak within a few hours. In the majority of cases the paralysis appears as an isolated finding without demonstrable cause. The eye on the affected side cannot be closed and its waters excessively. The lips are displaced toward the healthy side and the corner of the mouth sags. "No proof of bacterial or viral infection has yet been adduced, and the actual pathogenesis remains unknown" (Kunkle 1950:1493). Treatment usually consists of kneading and friction on the afflicted side (Goodall-Copestake 1926:225).

I prepared simplified descriptions of ordinary hemiplegia, multiple or disseminated sclerosis, shaking palsy or Parkinson's disease, and Bell's palsy, neuro-muscular disorders which all share some symptoms in common, and read them to Sanapia for her reaction. She immediately chose the account of Bell's palsy as a description of ghost sickness, even suggesting that I had based the description on information with which she had supplied me.

The medical descriptions of Bell's palsy describe the facial paralysis present in ghost sickness; however, in these accounts no mention is made of a concomitantly occurring contraction, spasm, or paralysis of the hands and arms, a symptom which from Sanapia's accounts occurs in many cases of ghost sickness. The emotion of fear, a key theme in the accounts of actual ghost contagion, offers a clue to the etiology of the affliction of the hands and arms. Dr. Gail Neely (1968) offered the suggestion that fear or emotional shock is one of the major causes of hyperventilation, or highly irregular, abnormally rapid respiration. Schottstaedt (1960: 48–51) supports Neely's suggestion and adds:

> Hyperventilation deserves special emphasis because of its importance in giving rise to symptoms. . . . This process ultimately results in a state of respiratory alkalosis with effects throughout the body. Many sensations result from this chemical derangement. . . . If hyperventilation continues long enough, spasms of the hand and feet (tetany), a feeling of being paralyzed, and actual loss of consciousness may occur. . . . Any of these manifestations may arouse fear; the more dramatic ones ordinarily do.
>
> In addition, an anxious person often has irregular respiration, which may become sufficiently severe to produce all of the manifestations of hyperventilation. The overt behavior is usually avoidance, ranging from a readiness or desire for flight to actual running away.

Medical descriptions of tetany, which, as Schottstaedt mentioned, can be caused by hyperventilation, follow Sanapia's description of the hands in ghost sickness to the letter. Aub (1951:1275) writes:

The hands become stiff, with rigid fingers. The thumb is markedly adducted and partially covered by the stiff fingers, which are usually bent only at their metacarpophalangeal joints. The palm of the hand is hollowed, while the wrist and elbow are flexed.

It is significant that Sanapia's methods of doctoring ghost sickness follow the treatment by white doctors for Bell's palsy and hyperventilation. Her rationale for her method of treatment is not similar, but the actual results of the behavior which she initiates are. She applies her mouth to the patient's face in an attempt to suck the illness from the individual. She also applies liquid medicines to the face area and draws her Medicine feather over the skin in the afflicted area. This could constitute the "gentle massage," "kneading of the cheek muscles," and "gentle friction" prescribed by Kunkel (1950:1493–1494) and Goodall-Copestake (1926:225) for treatment of Bell's palsy. When Sanapia turns her attention to treating the contorted hands, her method, in general, follows that which Dr. Neely states that he utilizes to relieve the symptoms of hyperventilation. She drapes a towel or piece of cloth over the patient's face and directs him to inhale the pungent smoke produced by smoldering medicines. During this phase of treatment she croons to the patient and gently reassures him that his condition will be cured. Neely stresses that the calm reassurance of the patient suffering from hyperventilation was a necessary part of the treatment. He also temporarily places a bag or some sort of facial covering over the patient's mouth and nose to impede the invidiual's intake of oxygen and force the recirculation of carbon dioxide. He also notes that smelling salts or ammonia can be used to further decrease the patient's attempts at excessively deep and rapid breathing.

A Psychogenic Hypothesis

In an attempt to discover an organic or static description of ghost sickness it was found that the types of disorders which most thoroughly describe ghost sickness are all highly suspect as to their being more organic than more functional in nature. The particular reasons why this hypothesis was suggested prior to the discussion of Bell's palsy and hyperventilation were based on the noted similarity in age, sex, and general personality type of the ghost victims and the fact that though the rules for ghost avoidance are extremely simple and obvious, certain individuals still apparently voluntarily violate these rules with full knowledge of the predicted consequences. The discussion of Bell's palsy and hyperventilation added further evidence for the role of psychological phenomenon, for example, the emotion of fear, desire for avoidance, shock, emotional strain, pressure, and the therapeutic value of reassurance in the treatment of hyperventilation.

Two concepts of psychosomatic medicine must be mentioned and their utility evaluated before proceeding further. These concepts are "conversion reaction" and "vegetative neurosis." A conversion symptom is a symbolic expression of a well-defined emotional content, while a vegetative neurosis is the physiological accompaniment of constant, periodically recurring emotional states rather than an expression of an emotional state (Alexander 1948:7).

Heuristically, the concept of vegetative neurosis is disappointing for our purposes. It leads us nowhere, for it contains no aids to determine the meaning of expression, the expressive "why" of ghost sickness, for example. A conversion reaction (synonym: conversion hysteria), however, is a symbolic expression of a specific emotional state. It is essentially an unusual form of communication. A mode of symbolic communication, to function, must possess meaning for the group, that is, the relationship of the symbol to the referent must be accepted by group consensus. Thus, if it can be established that ghost sickness is a conversion reaction in Comanche society, the suggestion can be made that it acts as a form of communication. If we can identify the referents to the symbology being employed in this communication, we can perhaps decipher the message and determine the psychogenic roots of ghost sickness.

A person with conversion hysteria substitutes a symptom for a psychological conflict. "For example, a girl of eighteen goes blind in an examination, thinking, 'I don't see how I can pass this,' and four years later goes blind again when her bridegroom is ordered overseas." (Cobb 1950:1514). Physiologically, conversion is no different from any normal method of expressing emotion, such as weeping, laughing, and blushing. Hysterical conversion, however, is motivated by unconscious impulses. Motor paralysis is the most common symptom in such instances. It is also noteworthy that conversion symptoms often imitate organic illness, that is, they represent the patient's notion of disease process.

Thus, it can be seen that the physiological nature of ghost sickness, paralysis of voluntary muscles, can be considered as at least similar to the general complexion of the major manifestations of conversion reactions. However, the nature of the precipitating factors involved remains a problem. What is the content of the "psychological conflict, unconscious alien impulse, or unbearable idea" (West 1962:94) which could cause a conversion reaction in a Comanche individual resulting in ghost sickness.

The Victim of the Ghost

In my study of the Comanche ghost-sickness victim, I noticed that a definite attempt at emulative adaptation to white society which failed, the unendurable psychological state of cultural marginality, and an extremely intense desire for reintegration with the more traditionally oriented group were the three most prevalent themes preceding the onslaught of ghost sickness. The victim usually sprang from the traditional group; therefore he desired reintegration with that particular group. Also, though the victim may have initially naively desired to interact in only one institution of white society, usually the economic system, his traditional group automatically defines him totally out of their category. Absolute outcasting from the traditional group is not what really happens in every case; however, it seems to be what the ghost-sickness victim thinks happened. The ghost-sickness victim will feel extremely anxious under the conditions outlined. He does not consciously accept that he has done anything to deserve the negative treatment which he feels he is receiving from both white and Indian society. Anger toward white society and guilt feelings, perhaps based on his rejection of the Indian way, might arise in him. He has been judged inadequate by both the white and the Indian worlds. He belongs nowhere. An individual in this situation must act.

The next problem he must face is the method by which reintegration with the native group can be accomplished. For this type of individual it is not easy, for he desires to become totally like the group which he once rejected. He must dramatically convince himself as well as his traditional group that he is an Indian, that he belongs. Simply returning to the family locale and indulging in self-conscious identification with ceremonial forms, for example, is not enough. He must have no doubts about his adequacy as an Indian. He can no longer tolerate ambivalency, and he must be as acceptable to himself as he is to his parent group.

Indian-ness and Ghost Sickness

In contemporary Comanche society there is only one trait which is unequiv-ocally and exclusively Indian—the ability to contract ghost sickness. "Blood" means nothing because of the great degree of intermarriage with other tribes and the Comanche's long-standing custom of incorporating white and Mexican captives into the family structure. Non-Indians can take part in Peyotism, dance in cere-monial dancing societies, and speak the Comanche language. A non-Indian, however, cannot incur ghost sickness. Therefore, to Comanches, someone who contracts ghost sickness must be a "real Indian."

The Efficiency of Ghost Sickness

Ghost sickness possesses several other characteristics which make it a very efficient disorder for the potential victim. It is socially visible; the ghost-sickness victim can wear the badge of his true Indian-ness on his face. It can only be cured by a native doctor. In this way the victim, by becoming the patient of the native doctor, states his faith in an extremely ancient Comanche institution. Because this doctor will no doubt cure him, the victim's faith is substantiated. Further, the Comanche community comes to the aid, succor, and support of the victim of the ghost—the common enemy. Associated with this fact is the function of the physical ugliness which the ghost victim possesses. By being so "pitiable," he can direct the course of his reintegration to a great degree through the Comanche institutionalized patterns of generosity and kindness to individuals who are in a pitiable condition. In this physical condition he can make personal demands which he could not make and expect to be carried out if he were not so afflicted. Also, since ghost-sickness symptoms are admirably suited to the requirements of con-version reactions, the affliction is manifestly ideal for the particular nature of the intolerable emotional state possessed by the potential ghost victim.

Precipitating Factors

The precipitating factors to ghost sickness need not be as externally dramatic as those thus far presented. The drama and the trauma of these factors dwell within the psychological makeup of the particular individual involved. The contraction of ghost sickness can function as a psychic reminder to a Comanche that he is a Comanche. It can serve to reaffirm his ethnic identity. It may be a self-inflicted punishment by a native-oriented Comanche who begins to doubt his traditional culture. Ghost sickness has also served to dramatically solve generational tensions. A young person contracts ghost sickness to signal acquiescence to the parent generation's demands. However, all these factors are ultimately related to the disruptive influences of acculturation with the dominant white society.

The recently developed Comanche ghost complex appears to be a means by which certain Comanche individuals can circumvent the psychological impasses which have appeared as a result of the twentieth-century Comanche life situation. It is particularly beneficial for the traditional group for several reasons. If a Comanche individual chooses this means of relief, he is committed to return to the traditionalist fold. The ghost complex might be viewed as a selective net which the traditional group has thrown around itself. Those Comanches who are drawn into the conditions which lead to the emotional states in which they would unconsciously choose ghost sickness as an "out" are usually relatively sensitive and intelligent individuals and therefore valuable as group members. They would have to fully and traumatically feel their intolerable cultural and psychological position prior to ghost sickness. Those Comanches who approach these same conditions and who fail to react to them, or acculturate, or turn to such relief as alcoholism, would not be very valuable social components to the traditional group in any case. This "net" operates to more effectively retain the big fish, while it lets the little fish run.

The fact that men are afflicted by ghost sickness more often than women could be explained by several factors, particularly, the greater degree of independence ideally expected of men, coupled with the real economic dependence of men; in many cases, dependence on women. Women are more effectively controlled by the primary group, while Comanche men are expected to "act like men" in the face of economic difficulties and a white society which does not recognize them as men.

Change in Behavior

The behavior change exhibited by ghost-sickness victims from prior to the onset of ghost sickness until the termination of the cure corresponds with one of the desires which stimulated the victim to ghost sickness in the first place—total identification with the traditional group. They become model traditional-oriented group members, while, prior to ghost sickness, they behaved in a manner considered erratic, bizarre, or "crazy" by these Comanches.

Ghost Sickness and Witch Sickness

Sanapia's great success in curing ghost-sickness victims appears to give further support to the idea of the psychogenesis of ghost sickness. Then again, she would also be attributed with success in curing a transient unilateral facial paralysis of an organic genesis which ran its course during the time of treatment or within a suitable time span after treatment. Of course, they both support the same conclusion to the Comanches: Sanapia can cure ghost sickness. However, if Sanapia is successful in curing ghost sickness, why does she enjoy a relative lack of success in curing the victims of witchcraft when the symptomatic manifestations of the two are practically identical? Once again, as in the discussion of ghost sickness, a valuable clue is suggested by looking at standardization in the age and sex of the victims of the witch. The institution of witchcraft will be more thoroughly surveyed in Chapter 5. It seems most appropriate that the etiology of witchcraft symptoms should be discussed at this juncture since we are approaching the question of Sanapia's cultural function as curer of afflictions believed by the Comanches to be magically or supernaturally instigated.

The overwhelming majority of Comanche witch victims are infants, rarely more than several years of age. Therefore, we must base our attempt at explanation of the symptoms of witch sickness on an organic disorder which corresponds to the symptoms displayed by the witched victim. The medical literature presents an account of a disorder which corresponds in type to the symptoms present in ghost sickness and witch sickness, but which is limited, with rare exceptions, to infants less than two years of age. This neuromuscular disorder, tetany, also exhibits two symptoms by which Sanapia conceptually differentiates between witch sickness and ghost sickness by the degree of their severity. Sanapia points out that though witch- and ghost-sickness victims demonstrate similar modes of contortion, the witch victim's contortions appear most often in spasmodic fashion, while this trait is less marked in ghost sickness. Also, the peculiar contractions of the hands and arms, described in discussing ghost sickness, are more prevalent in cases of witch sickness. Further, two major causes of tetany in infants result from inadequate calcium intake and vitamin D deficiency, dietary lacks which could easily occur in the relatively poor environment in which many Comanche infants are reared.

Aub (1951:1275) mentions that signs of tetany will result from alkalosis of various origins, such as hyperventilation. The relationship of the emotion of fear to hyperventilation is noteworthy. Although the infant does not understand that he is the target of the witch, his parents do. Perhaps the parents' increased anxiety over the symptoms of tetany, which they could associate with witchcraft, only acts to increase anxiety in the infant, thus more readily acting to increase the possibility of hyperventilation. It is a common observation that the emotional state of parents can affect the emotional state of their infant children.

Because of the suggested differences in etiology of ghost sickness and witch sickness, Sanapia's success with ghost sickness and relative lack of success in curing witch sickness is understandable. She can relieve some of the symptoms of witch sickness through her ability to ease the anxiety of the parents and therefore decrease the anxiety which is communicated to the child. However, Sanapia cannot alleviate certain factors, perhaps of an environmental nature, which have caused tetany. It is also significant that with witch victims, because of their age, Sanapia is unable to communicate. In discussing the actual treatment of ghost sickness, it was seen that psychotherapeutic traits in her behavior toward her patient are ubiquitous.

Sanapia, Ghosts, and Ghost Sickness

A great amount of time has been spent in discussing ghosts, ghost sickness, and the suggested causes of ghost sickness because of this complex's close association to Sanapia's role in Comanche society. As an eagle doctor, Sanapia's special thaumaturgic power is believed to be her ability to counteract or defeat the ghost's malevolent influences on living men. Because of the nature of the symptoms associated with ghost sickness and because of their probable psychogenic etiology, she is almost always successful in treating the victim of the ghost. If the affliction which her patient possesses is an organically based transient unilateral facial paralysis, it will disappear of its own accord when it runs its course; and if the disorder is hysterically induced, the patient actually cures himself, while Sanapia more or less functions as a symbol to the patient that the time for his cure is at hand. Of course, the psychotherapeutic value of her method of curing cannot be minimized, and perhaps it could be said that the emotional state which she induces in her hysterical patient functions as a trigger for his self-healing.

Sanapia's most important overt function in contemporary Comanche society is as a symbol of the Comanche's ability to withstand the attacks of the ghosts. She also serves as the necessary key to the psychological reintegration of marginal Comanches who have "employed" the ghost-sickness conversion reaction. As long as Sanapia, or other eagle doctors, stand as a source of cure, Comanche individuals can contract ghost sickness as a means of relieving certain intolerable emotional states. This could also serve to explain the longevity of the institution of the Comanche eagle doctor, while the other kinds of Comanche native doctors have long since ceased to exist. The human disorder associated with the eagle doctor's particular brand of specialization, ghost sickness, has only increased with the acculturation of the Comanche people, while the specialties of the other varieties of Comanche doctors have been usurped during this same process. It is ironic that acculturation, while actively corroding the overall complexion of traditional Comanche culture, has also served to revive and augment the important function of a symbol of traditional Comanche culture, the Medicine woman.

5

Witchcraft and
the Conceptualization of Illness

Black Magic

WITCHCRAFT and the conceptualization of illness, two seemingly separate areas, are best discussed together because Sanapia's notions of witchcraft present the most obvious examples of her manner of conceptualizing human illness and its causes. The variety of Comanche witchcraft described here is carried out by one of the major methods of the classic witch, a ritual of malevolent imitative magic; however, its perpetrator is not a witch but a shaman who has only temporarily utilized his supernatural powers and knowledge or ritual for purposes of evil. I will use the noun and the verb forms of the word "witch" as my Comanche informants do, keeping this distinction in mind. E. Adamson Hoebel (1940:85) writes: "The Comanche made no basic distinction between a Medicine man and a sorcerer. Medicine was a two-edged sword. It could cut for good or evil."

Witchcraft is an extremely delicate area to investigate among contemporary Comanches. In the sense that the term is presently used among Comanches, it is synonymous with the most diabolical kind of murder. A Medicine woman who was notorious for her acts of malevolent magic has died only within the last several years, and it appears that many Comanches now look upon Sanapia, the only Medicine woman still living, not only with a calculated respect but also with suspicion and a certain amount of fear. The label "witch" was never directly applied by my informants to Sanapia, though some Comanches noted her quick temper and stated that they knew Comanches who were afraid to associate with her lest they arouse her temper and run the risk of having it directed at them.

Sanapia quite naturally denies that she would witch another person, though she is evasive concerning the possibility of her potential to witch if she so desired. When this specific subject presented itself in the course of our discussion, her response could be predicted. In every instance of a question which alluded to the possibility of her utilization of her powers to harm others she drew on the

Bible for her response and for material to construct what she felt would be her evasion of the point of the question. This is an example of the manner in which Sanapia has organized elements and sentiments of the three supernaturalistic systems which affect her life into a supportive and cohesive whole. The following quotation is standard of her manner of responding to the many questions which were directed to her concerning her potential to execute witchcraft. It should be noted that in the example given, she indirectly admits to a belief that she is at least capable of witchcraft. This also was a recurring element in all her responses to questions on this subject.

> I don't think about it much, because the Bible tells me not to kill. I'll be punished if I die. God's going to do that to me. You can't steal too. Can't steal from nobody. That's what I learn in the Bible. Don't steal from nobody. Stealing is bad and people could get in trouble for it. [Proceeds to tell a story about a thief.]

Sanapia is, however, quite knowledgeable as to a Comanche method of witchcraft, a method which, in my opinion, is strictly the province of the eagle doctor. A few years before the death of the Medicine woman previously mentioned, she was invited to live with Sanapia. This fact is still very present in the minds of some Comanches who continue to allude to this when they are discussing the fear which Sanapia arouses in some of her people. Sanapia states that doctors have a special obligatory bond which motivated her to offer assistance to the older woman who, at the time, was experiencing economic and health difficulties. She does admit that during this time she learned very much about witchcraft from the older doctor, who was also an eagle doctor.

Reasons for the Use of Witchcraft

There are, of course, a variety of reasons why a *puhakut* would resort to witchcraft. The most common reason in Sanapia's opinion is jealousy, although a Medicine practitioner can also be commissioned to use his powers and knowledge of witching ritual for evil. There is also the instance in which a Medicine man is told in a dream that he will be able to save the life of his patient if he first takes another's life. Sanapia states that the latter two instances are rare in modern times and that most witchcraft victims whom she has doctored have been witched because they, or more likely their parents, inspired jealousy in certain old people who possessed *puha* and who knew how to witch. It is significant that in the several accounts of witching which Sanapia has reported, she always laid the blame for the act on old people and in almost every case on old women. It is also relevant to note that five of the six accounts which Sanapia has supplied concerning victims of witchcraft which she has doctored have been infants of less than two years of age. Sanapia, however, insists that anyone of any age can be the victim of the witch. When questioned concerning the high rate of infants as witchcraft victims, she replied that some old women whose children have left them become jealous of the children of other women and to punish the younger women attempt to kill their children.

Sanapia feels that the incidents of witchcraft are very rare and are occurring less frequently as the older people of the tribe pass away. In her career as a doctor, a period spanning approximately thirty years, Sanapia reports only six cases of which she has had personal knowledge, though she points out that when she was younger, there were more doctors who could be approached for aid by a witchcraft victim.

The last case of this kind which Sanapia treated occurred two months after I had established rapport with her. It was the first case of witchcraft which she had doctored in four years. This was fortunate for the purposes of my investigation, for Sanapia's full attention was on the subject, and I was also able to obtain an account of the manner in which she doctored her niece's child, the victim of the witch. Before proceeding with a description of the doctoring of a witched individual, I would like to discuss a method of witchcraft known by Sanapia.

A Method of Witchcraft

When a *puhakut* has decided to witch someone, he first spends four days fasting and praying that what he is about to wish will come to pass. These four days are not as rigorously observed as the four days of "vision quest." Fasting is not total, and though he should be outside during the day where he has privacy, he is free to return to his home at night. When he goes to pray, the *puhakut* is only allowed to take water and Bull Durham tobacco and corn shucks for rolling cigarettes. He must also be at his chosen place of prayer before sunrise to make his morning prayers to the sun. This is the first of many elements in this method of witchcraft which strongly suggests that it was or is the method of the eagle doctors. Sanapia, of course, denies this.

After the period of preparation, the *puhakut* laces a short length of buckskin through his flesh and ties it in a knot, thus forming a loose loop about an inch in diameter which is attached to the flesh. This piece of buckskin can be placed anywhere on the body, though Sanapia states that it is usually visible. She is not unaware of the psychological affect such a display can have.

Maybe someone sees him like that . . . with that buckskin, they might get scared and stop doing what's making him mad. That's what I think. I ask some old man that had that when I was little what he was doing and he didn't say nothing to me. My grandmother get after me for talking to him and she told me about that part. Later I heard of it around here.

The time between the first stage of the act of witchcraft and the execution of the final stages is indeterminate in length. Perhaps, as Sanapia suggests, if the display of the buckskin loop frightens the potential victim enough, the actions which are aggravating the *puhakut* may cease, and the final stage of the witching need not occur. During this time the wearer of the buckskin loop tells no one who his potential victim might be, and it is considered a breach of etiquette to quiz him on the subject. There is also the element of fear present since the *puhakut*, though prepared to witch, does not name his victim until the final stage of witchcraft, and thus any untoward actions by an individual may draw the *puhakut*'s pent-up resolve in a direction which could be decided by him on the spur of the moment. Sanapia likens the *puhakut*, during this phase of witchcraft, to a bomb which could be detonated at the slightest touch.

The final stage of witchcraft is initiated by sunrise on the selected day and is completed by sunset on the same day. The *puhakut* takes a white eagle plume and, puncturing the base of the rib, inserts a length of buckskin approximately 12 inches long. The buckskin is tied so that the plume dangles tip down from this buckskin strand. Immediately before sunrise, carrying this one specially prepared item, the *puhakut* goes off by himself to perform his witchcraft. He secures the plume from the branch of a tree in such a manner that it will be hidden from the view of a possible passerby but so it can move freely at the dictates of the wind. He then sits beneath the plume and begins to pray for the death of his victim. As he prays, he makes before him in the soil a small replica of a grave and prays that when the plume finally breaks free from its tether, the object of his prayers will die and enter the grave which has been prepared for him. At sunset the *puhakut* returns to his home, his witchcraft completed. He wears the buckskin loop until the death of his victim, at which time he cuts it from his skin, burns it, and throws the ashes into the nearest running water.

Kardiner (1945:67) writes that a Comanche who thought he was going to be witched or who had been witched could pay the doctor who was responsible to remove the "spell." Sanapia denies this and emphasizes that one of the particularly horrible things about witchcraft is that it cannot be stopped once it is set in motion. A doctor can sometimes cure the witch's victim once the witchcraft has been actualized, but nothing can be done by a doctor before the symptoms appear in the victim. She feels that the majority of witching situations never reach the final stage. In her opinion the buckskin loop advertisement of the witch usually persuades the potential victim to cease his misbehavior before the witch finally and irrevocably sets his black magic into operation. Sanapia also states that this is used as a form of blackmail by some Comanches.

Sanapia refers to this final stage of witchcraft as "shooting the feather." She states that the witch causes the eagle plume to enter the body of the victim at the moment it breaks free from its tether. The feather enters the victim immediately below the surface of the skin and proceeds to move rapidly over the entire body area, causing the physical symptoms associated with witchcraft. It finally lodges in some area of the victim's body, where it will eventually cause his death if it is not removed by a doctor who possesses the Medicine required to counteract its influence.

It is significant that the method of witchcraft as related by an eagle doctor would have as its principle ritual an eagle plume which is prepared and utilized in such a manner as to make it as much like an eagle as possible: It is placed very high in a tree, and it is attached to the tree in such a manner that it will be able to move freely and naturally at the motion of the wind. This follows from the imitative and sympathetic mystical rapport an eagle doctor possess with his supernatural patron, the eagle; and it suggests that possibly this method of witchcraft is, or was, in the form of a special Medicine solely possessed by doctors with eagle power and that doctors who possessed a different supernatural patron would also possess different method of witchcraft. The emphasis on prayers to the sun is also relevant.

The Symptoms of Witch Sickness

Sanapia feels that the symptoms exhibited by an individual who has been witched are unmistakable. Such a person feels tired and listless and is unable to retain food. He wants to sleep continually and usually suffers from fever. The unique symptom of witchcraft, according to Sanapia, is excessive perspiration on the top of the victim's head, perspiration which the victim cannot feel and which can be felt only by a doctor possessing the proper Medicine. She believes that this localized fever is caused by "foamy stuff" which accumulates under the skin surface at the top of the head. The foamy stuff is, in turn, caused by the magically toxic witch's feather. Also occurring are symptoms which are very similar to the unilateral facial paralysis which appears with ghost sickness. In the case of witchcraft, however, the victim's eyes do not water, he does not salivate excessively, and the contortions of the face, hands, and arms occur in spasmodic fashion rather than the constant state of paralysis found with ghost sickness. In both cases the contortions of the face are felt to be caused by pockets of foamy stuff which accumulate under the skin.

Sanapia feels that ghost and witch sickness are the most difficult types of sickness to treat because both are essentially unnatural and malevolent. In contrast, pneumonia, for example, is a natural sickness which does not possess the supernatural tenacity of illnesses which are backed by the supernatural and malevolent resolve of a ghost or witch. Thus with ghost and witch sickness, Sanapia must not only cure the symptomatic effects of these illnesses but must also act to neutralize the malevolent supernatural power which is somehow contiguous with these symptoms.

Treatment of Witch Sickness

When Sanapia doctors a victim of witchcraft, she utilizes *təpinatsu*, *ekapokowa:pi*, *kusiwɜna*, her Medicine feather, glass slivers, charcoal from the peyote drum, and her sucking horn. She prepares a thin paste of *kusiwɜna* and applies it to the area of the patient's body which she feels to be the place where the feather is located. *Təpinatsu* and *ekapokowa:pi* are deposited on live coals to produce medicine smoke which is wafted over the patient to induce healing.

The procedure begins before sunrise on the first day of treatment when Sanapia makes her morning prayers to the rising sun. She begins treatment proper when she feels all conditions to be favorable. Exactly what criteria Sanapia uses to judge when the time is right to begin treatment would be difficult to outline. A good portion of such a feeling would naturally be highly personal. Some conditions which would be negative influences on Sanapia's decision to begin treatment might be barking dogs, the sudden appearance of visitors, an infant's crying, or a sudden change of weather. Sanapia would consider barking dogs or a sudden change of weather as negative omens. The appearance of visitors or the crying of an infant would simply be distracting to her.

When she initiates treatment, she first prays over the patient and fans smoke produced by the *təpinatsu* and *ekapokowa:pi* over him. After her first prayer, in which she calls on her powers to assist her, she takes her charcoal medicine and draws a circle around the area on the patient's body in which she feels the feather is located to prevent the feather's escape to another area of the body. Next, she makes several incisions in the area of the circle and applies a thin paste of *kusiwɜna* over the incisions. She then fans her medicine smoke over this area and begins her attempt to suck the feather from the patient's body.

As blood, sucked from the area of incisions, collects in her sucking horn or in her mouth, she deposits it on a white paper plate which she keeps near her. The entire procedure of cutting, applying medicine, fanning, and attempting to remove the feather by suction continues until Sanapia has removed the feather or has come to the conclusion that her powers are not sufficient to cure the patient. When and if the feather appears in the plate of blood she shows the plate to the patient, or the patient's parents, and pronounces him cured; and, after giving the patient a final blessing, the treatment is completed.

The word "appears," when used in connection with the removal of the witch's feather, must be understood in a special sense. Sanapia does not state that she removes a real feather. She reports that the Comanche words she uses when exhibiting the plate of blood to the patient after the "removal of the feather" means that the effects of the feather have been removed. She feels that the witch can project the evil potential of the plume into the body of the victim, though the feather itself is not magically injected into the vitcim. Sanapia doctors to alleviate the physical symptoms which result from the magically injected malevolent essence of the eagle plume utilized in the act of witchcraft. This notion of transmitting the essence of an object into a person was mentioned in the discussion of Sanapia's doctoring of ghost sickness. During her doctoring in the specially arranged peyote meeting, Sanapia attempted to transmit the pliable qualities of the wet drumhead to the patient's face. She also applied the stone peyote drum "bosses" to the patient's face so that, through her powers, the positive qualities of these stones—firmness and stability—could be injected into the patient's contorted face to heal him. Just as Sanapia attempted to inflict positive powers from their source to a patient, so could she use her powers to inject negative essences of an object into an individual. But what is the particular malevolent essence of an eagle plume which can be utilized to witch? As we discuss the manner in which Sanapia conceptualizes the nature and cause of human illness, the answer will present itself.

Concepts of Illness

Sanapia employs three basic notions as foundations in her conceptualization of the nature of illness. The first of these may be stated: Things in rapid and erratic motion or rapid and erratic motion itself are intrinsically dangerous to the human body. It is pertinent that Kardiner (1945:66) mentions that the Comanches thought of diseases not as material objects but as kinds of insects, living things, which had somehow gotten into the body.

The second of these basic ideas is that virtually all human physiological malfunction is caused by the swelling of certain body tissues, liquids, or specific organs; and the third of these conceptual foundations is that illness in the human body manifests itself materially in the form of a toxic liquid which has its center of production in the immediate area of the abnormal swelling or which is the cause of the swelling in the body of the sick individual. In the majority of cases this threefold scheme can be stated: Something moving rapidly or erratically in the body has caused an area of the body to become swollen. This swollen area is producing a toxic liquid which, if removed from the body, will relieve the symptoms of the illness. The cause of the illness is destroyed by the supernatural power of Sanapia or by the medicines which she has endorsed with extraordinary potential.

In Sanapia's description of the execution of the final stages of witchcraft, she made great note of the necessity of using an eagle plume which must be prepared and attached to the tree branch in such a manner that it will be free to dance and flutter with any breezes that should contact it. She also gestured rapidly to depict how the plume would react to the wind when she described the plume's placement in the tree branch. The reason why a feather is not used is that it would not move properly in the wind. The erratic movement of the plume is essential in witchcraft. In addition, the magical feather, upon entering the body of the victim, moves rapidly over the body, and it is only after Sanapia has magically surrounded it by enclosing it in a circle of charcoal that the feather's movement is made impossible.

Sanapia describes an extreme form of insanity as that state in which the affected individual usually twitches, jerks, and "runs around crazy." Then again, when describing the whirlwind guise of the ghost, she made the point that the whirlwinds move around very quickly and erratically. When she describes the behavior of poisons injected by certain insects and poisonous spiders, she states that this poison, upon entering the body, turns into "eggs" which race wildly over the body. In sign language, Sanapia indicates "sickness" by a rapid, quivering movement of the hands over the chest area. This sign for sickness is noted for the Plains area generally by Tomkins (1926:51). More examples could be listed; however, I am attempting to state several slightly different circumstances in which rapid and/or erratic motion, or some variant of this theme, was considered in a definitely negative manner when considered in the context of its relation to the human body. Thus it can be seen that the malevolent essence of the witching feather which is injected into the victim's body is rapid and erratic motion.

The notion of swelling is included in practically every description of illness which Sanapia relates. It is also significant that one of her major medicines is *bekwinatsu*, or swelling medicine. In Sanapia's opinion, ghost sickness, pneumonia, rheumatism, asthma, headaches, vertigo, constipation, and a number of other human complaints have swelling as their central pathological core. As stated previously, the swelling is either produced by or produces a toxic liquid, usually referred to by Sanapia as foamy stuff, which by its nature expands in the body. It is this liquid or the swelling that produces this liquid, which causes the symptoms of illnesses such as those just mentioned, but not the illness itself. The foamy stuff, the only tangible and manipulatable manifestation of illness, is removed from the body by the *puhakut* by suction or by being driven out.

Sanapia states that she never removes an object from the patient's body claiming that she has removed the sickness, although she remembers that her mother did this. Sanapia feels that she cures by removing the poison, or foamy stuff, present in the patient's body and by using her supernatural powers to assure that through her prayers the patient may live a long and healthy life. In other words, the supernatural or unknown causes of the patient's illnesses are banished through her prayers.

Sanapia describes a healthy body as one which possesses a balance and calm throughout all its tissues, liquids, and organs. When something causes this balance and calm to be disrupted, sickness results. Some foreign agent moving in a rapid and erratic manner through the body is definitely unsettling to the body's parts. Swollen areas displace tissues, organs and body liquids, also unsettling the body balance. Foamy stuff irritates the body generally.

Sanapia is persistent in her comments that she never actually removes a real feather from the body of the victim of a witch; however, she states that most Comanches who come to her for this treatment believe she does.

> They ain't got no power . . . never learned them ways, so how do they know? They can think what they want to think. I get them well, or their little baby. That's what they come here for, and I do it so they can believe what they want. If it makes them happy, let them think what they like. I don't care about it myself.

From Sanapia's description of the doctoring of the witched victim, it can be seen that she does not exert herself to make him, or his parents, think any other way about the reality of the feather in his body. In other words, she never reports that there is not a feather in him, and all her behavior during the treatment only lends support to the patient's belief that there is a real feather present in his body.

Another aspect of the *puhakut*'s treatment of witchcraft victims is suggested by Kardiner (1945:67). He writes that Comanche doctors were able to identify the individual responsible for the witching during the treatment of the one who had been witched.

With regard to Sanapia's niece's child, Sanapia said that she knew who had witched the girl but did not tell the mother for fear of frightening her. Sanapia does not suggest that any supernatural talents are involved in the ability to identify the witch. Since Sanapia believes that witchcraft can only be operated by those with a high degree of *puha*, the field of possibilities is immediately narrowed. She evaluates the community in which the witch's victim lives and, through a process of elimination, selects the witch. She does not make her choice known for fear of frightening the victim or his parents, as has been mentioned, and also because she feels that if her accusations are made public, it would only cause further dissension among the Comanche people. She feels that there is enough tension among the Comanches without adding accusations of witchcraft.

The Contemporary Situation

This chapter has dealt with Sanapia's treatment of a victim who has been witched by the magical insertion of the malevolent essence of an eagle plume. Sanapia doctors also among the Wind River Shoshone, southern Cheyenne, southern and northern Arapaho, Kiowa, Kiowa-Apache, Ponca, Creek, and Fort Sill Apache, as well as the Comanche; and thus she has confronted cases of witchcraft other than the variety which has been described in this chapter. Her general approach to a cure, however, is similar in all cases. She feels that the body of the victim has been put out of balance by some tangible or intangible entity; therefore, to correct the abnormal condition, she works to remove that which is causing this physiological disequilibrium.

Given the antagonistic feelings beween the northern and southern Comanches and the fact that patterns of witchcraft exist, it would seem that there would be a high rate of intergroup witchcraft, at least being directed by the northerners. This does not appear to be the case, a major reason being that the southerners generally do not respond. They consider witches and witchcraft merely superstitious beliefs, or, at best, nonexistent in modern times. A further possible explanation of this lack of intergroup witchcraft is the special distribution of the Comanche bands—the more traditionally oriented bands cluster in the north and northwest of the Comanche area while the more fully acculturated band members are found in the south and southwest. There may be as many as 40 miles separating members of these two groups. Therefore, there is no necessity for daily social interaction between members of the opposing "tribes," which could reduce the generalized hostilities to more intense and socially unsettling personal conflict, thus better facilitating the desire and the opportunity for the execution of witchcraft.

Witchcraft among contemporary Comanches is mainly intergenerational. Older men and women, feeling their life power fading, turn to malevolent magic in an attempt to augment their failing social prestige and to defend themselves against the more vital younger generation. The few cases of witchcraft which I was able to investigate among the Comanches followed this general pattern of essentially intergenerational jealousy and tension. This was also the basic rationale for witchcraft, especially between males, in the nomadic Comanche culture. In a society which emphasized physical prowess, the old and enfeebled were at a definite disadvantage. The older men could not join the younger in the prestigeful activities of war, sexual adventuring, and hunting, and they were therefore forced to turn to magic and supernatural means if they desired to continue their futile attempts to compete for social power and prestige with the younger men of the tribe. Since Comanche culture was not oriented to allow an individual to acquire prestige and position through material acquisition alone, this avenue was also denied the older men.

Factors in the Decline of Witchcraft

Perhaps a factor contributing to the lessening incidences of witchcraft, noted by Sanapia even in her own time, can be attributed to the fact that in the post-reservation period the older men of the tribe were able to acquire a certain economic power through such channels as land allotments and welfare, while at the same time the younger men were being denied their main traditional avenue to prestige—war. Thus a more tolerable balance developed between the prestige and social power levels of the young and the old. The woman, whose social position rose and fell with the male to whom she was attached, also acquired the benefits of this postreservation phenomenon. A woman could own land like a male, and with older women this became an attraction to the younger men, men perhaps born too late to take full advantage of the land allotments. Therefore, an older and economically more powerful woman could more successfuly compete with a younger woman for available males.

However, neither economic power nor supernatural methods can cause a woman to produce offspring after she has reached a certain advanced age. In a moment of anger or spite, a young Comanche woman's invectives directed toward an old woman will inevitably include a caustic reminder to the older woman of her "uselessness" as a woman. Sanapia and many of my female Comanche informants mentioned the potential dangers which a young woman exposes herself and her children to when she flaunts her offspring in front of an older woman whose children have left her. This, in Sanapia's opinion, is the reason for the high degree of witched infants and why Sanapia immediately accuses an old woman for the act of witchcraft.

Several other factors can be suggested as relevant to the decline of Comanche witchcraft. With the allotment of lands the various family units within the same band became more isloated and thus any possibility of an act which could motivate an individual to operate witchcraft against another member of that band became lessened as relatively forced social proximity, as was the case in the reservation period, became lessened among band members.

As the band's economic function was destroyed, the individual family units were compelled to become more independent. Thus, the older members of the Comanche extended families were necessarily allotted tasks as more jobs had to be handled by a smaller number of individuals. In this manner the older people served a valuable function to the group and were therefore able to retain a certain amount of prestige. Another factor which no doubt contributed to the raising of the prestige of older Comanches and therefore to the decline in witchcraft was the influence of Christianity with its stress on respect for the aged.

The suggestions which I have offered and which I feel are necessary for an understanding of the relative insignificance of witchcraft among contemporary Comanches are all ultimately rooted in the dynamics of acculturation. Witchcraft has disappeared as an effective means of social control among Comanches as its function has become obliterated by the changes brought about by acculturation with the dominant white society. Nothing served to directly replace the institution of Comanche witchcraft. This type of institution became meaningless as the very foundations for its existence were destroyed by the acculturative phenomenon which served to augment, equalize, and temporally lengthen, through essentially economic means, the levels of social power and prestige obtainable by all Comanche individuals.

Conclusion

Lack of Comparable Material

MANY OF THE PROBLEMS in evaluating the material presented in this book stem from the fact that there is little Comanche information with which to compare it. The information contained in Kardiner's (1945) discussion of Comanche culture is based on data supplied largely by Ralph Linton which he gathered with the Santa Fe group in 1933. Wallace and Hoebel's (1952) book is almost totally based on material obtained in 1933 by this same group. Therefore, practically all that is known of Comanche ethnography is based on the circumstances of several months in 1933. A further problem is that Sanapia, in her role as eagle doctor, is unique in contemporary Comanche society. There is no one with whom to compare her. This also means that there is no way to check the information which Sanapia supplied, except so far as it was the type which could be verified by other Comanches. Consistency in her responses to the same questions asked at various times and her desire that this study act as the "book of her Medicine way" are the only indications which can be suggested to support the high probability of her veracity in materials which could not be otherwise checked.

Inconsistencies

The inconsistencies between data presented by Sanapia and the materials presented by the authors who have written on Comanche notions of power, magic, and religion have been noted in the body of the text. Since any conclusions based on these differences would necessarily be spurious, I will not introduce them again in conclusion. It is enough to say that Sanapia's interpretation of her relation to the supernatural is consistent to her and to other Comanches. It would be futile and improper to discuss whether she is "right" or whether Wallace, Hoebel, and Kardiner are "right."

Sanapia, 1969.

The pervasive influence of acculturation is a fact which cannot be skirted, however, and perhaps it is at the core of the inconsistencies between Sanapia and the ethnographers of the early 1930s. Sanapia is particularly immediately affected by the changes wrought by acculturation and change because of the nature of her role. The notion of her "place" in Comanche society, plus the rigidly bound manner in which her behavior is directed by certain supernatural sanctions, forces her to react to change piecemeal. A Comanche not so bound as Sanapia to certain prescribed modes of behavior and thought can ebb and flow with the stimuli of acculturation. He can bend, withdraw, aggress, and withdraw again, while retaining a homogeneous and integrated self-concept. Sanapia, however, is relatively rigid and must react immediately lest her role structure be shattered.

Sanapia Prevails

To Sanapia, she is an eagle doctor first and foremost. Her whole life is bound in this role; therefore, its protection is extremely dear to her. Sanapia lives with compromise, rationalization, and intellectualization. Because of her functionalistic and pragmatic temperament, she must defend an institution which to her at times has little meaning in its particulars. Each new realization of acculturative changes stimulates her to attempt to fit this newly acquired realization into a nonantagonistic relationship to her role as Medicine woman. She knows that she must meet the threats of culture change directly if her institution is to continue to have meaning for Comanches who are reacting to acculturation.

In this manner she has incorporated elements and sentiments of Christianity and organized peyotism into her own religious structure in an attempt at compatibility with the religious atmosphere of her life situation. By accepting the basic tenets of Christianity and organized peyotism, she has also provided herself with further sources of supernatural powers. Sanapia has defined illness into "white" and "Indian" categories, thereby retaining her position in the overall medical structure of both cultures. She has borrowed words and concepts from the mass media to elaborate her views of certain aspects of physiology, health, and medicine. These are but a few examples. Sanapia, while anchoring her sentiments and loyalties in a traditional Comanche setting, has extended herself, through her concern with her profession, into the white culture.

Perhaps the most significant points this study has illustrated are the psychotherapeutic function which Sanapia possesses in contemporary Comanche culture and the psychological function of ghost sickness. Although it cannot be absolutely substantiated, it would appear that ghost sickness, in its present form, is a new arrival in Comanche society. Ghost sickness can be considered, in most cases, a conversion reaction whose negative emotional basis is founded in the cultural and personal confusion and tension produced by the increasingly efficient success of acculturation in corroding the traditional basis of Comanche society. It then appears that Sanapia is the curer of a dynamic and functional human disorder. She is not a specialist in the treatment of broken bones or gunshot wounds like a buffalo doctor, nor of rattlesnake bites, like a snake doctor; she is the curer of an illness which is psychodynamic in nature. As her people change, ghost sickness will no doubt change, and Sanapia and successive eagle doctors' interpretation of ghost sickness will also change. Sanapia treats the individual rather than a specific static human affliction; she is essentially a native psychiatrist. This dynamic flexibility has enable Comanche eagle doctors to exist long after the other varieties of Comanche native dotcors have had their function usurped by white doctors during the ongoing process of acculturation.

References

ALEXANDER, FRANZ, 1948, *Fundamentals of Psychoanalysis*. New York: Norton.

AUB, JOSEPH C., 1951, Tetany. In Russel L. Cecil and Robert F. Loeb (eds.), *A Textbook of Medicine*, pp. 1275–1277. Philadelphia: Saunders.

BASEHART, HARRY W., 1968, Personal communication. Albuquerque, N. M.: University of New Mexico.

BITTLE, WILLIAM E., 1967, Personal communication. Norman, Okla.: University of Oklahoma.

COBB, STANLEY, 1950, Introduction: Psychosomatic Medicine. In Russel L. Cecil and Robert F. Loeb (eds.), *A Textbook of Medicine*, pp. 1513–1514. Philadelphia: Saunders.

FREEMAN, DANIEL M. A., 1968, Personal communication. Philadelphia: University of Pennsylvania.

GOODALL-COPESTAKE, BEATRICE M., 1926, *The Theory and Practice of Massage*. New York: Hoeber.

HOEBEL, E. ADAMSON, 1960, *The Cheyennes*. New York: Holt, Rinehart and Winston, Inc.

JORDAN, JULIA A., 1968, Personal communication. Norman, Okla.: University of Oklahoma.

KEARNEY, THOMAS H., 1951, *Arizona Flora*. Berkeley, Calif.: University of California Press.

KROEBER, ALFRED L., 1939, *Cultural and Natural Areas of Native North America*. Berkeley, Calif.: University of California Press.

KUNKLE, CHARLES E., 1950, Bell's Palsy. In Russel L. Cecil and Robert F. Loeb (eds.), *A Textbook of Medicine*, pp. 1493–1494. Philadelphia: Saunders.

NEELY, GAIL M., 1968, Personal communication. Clinton, Okla.: Clinton Indian Hospital.

OPLER, MARVIN K., 1943, The Origins of Comanche and Ute. *American Anthropologist*, 45: 155–158.

SCHOTTSTAEDT, WILLIAM W., 1960, *Psychophysiological Approach in Medical Practice*. Chicago: Year Book Publishers, Inc.

TOMKINS, WILLIAM, 1926, *Universal Indian Sign Language of the Plains Indians of North America*. San Diego, Calif.

TRENHOLM, VIRGINIA C., and MAURINE COLE, 1964, *The Shoshoni: Sentinels of the Rockies*. Norman, Okla.: University of Oklahoma Press.

WEST, FRANKLIN H., 1962, Etiology and Mechanisms in Development of Conversion Reactions. In John H. Nodine and John H. Moyer (eds.), *Psychosomatic Medicine: The First Hahnemann Symposium*, pp. 84–100. Philadelphia: Lea and Febiger Press.

Recommended Reading

CARLSON, G. G., and V. H. JONES, 1940, Some Notes on the Uses of Plants by the Comanche Indians. In *Papers of the Michigan Academy of Science, Arts and Letters*, Vol. 25, pp. 517–542. Ann Arbor: University of Michigan Press.
A discussion of Comanche ethnobotany. More extensive than the specialized concerns of *Sanapia: Comanche Medicine Woman.*

HOEBEL, E. ADAMSON, 1940, The Political Organization and Law-Ways of the Comanche Indians. Memoir No. 54, the American Anthropological Association, Menasha, Wisconsin.
The best description and analysis of a Comanche institution.

KARDINER, ABRAM, 1945, The Comanches. In *Psychological Frontiers of Society.* New York: Columbia University Press.
Interesting both for its discussion of the roots of historic Comanche modal personality and for its analysis of the Comanche Basin-to-Plains cultural transition.

LOWIE, ROBERT, H., 1954, *Indians of the Plains.* Garden City, N. Y.: The Natural History Press.
A brief survey of the culture of the Plains Indians of North America.

RICHARDSON, RUPERT N., 1933, *The Comanche Barrier to South Plains Settlement.* Glendale, Calif.: Arthur H. Clark, Company.
An excellent reference for materials dealing with Comanche contact history. It is lacking, however, in useful information concerning Comanche culture.

WALLACE, ERNEST and E. ADAMSON HOEBEL, 1952, *The Comanches: Lords of the South Plains.* Norman, Okla.: University of Oklahoma Press.
The only ethnographic overview of the Comanche lifeway.